THE
PRECEDENCE
OF
ENGLISH BISHOPS:
AND THE
PROVINCIAL CHAPTER.

THE
PRECEDENCE
OF
ENGLISH BISHOPS:
AND THE
PROVINCIAL CHAPTER:

BY

CHR. WORDSWORTH, M.A.,

PREBENDARY OF LIDDINGTON IN LINCOLN CATHEDRAL CHURCH

CAMBRIDGE:
at the University Press
1906.

CAMBRIDGE
UNIVERSITY PRESS

University Printing House, Cambridge CB2 8BS, United Kingdom

Published in the United States of America by Cambridge University Press, New York

Cambridge University Press is part of the University of Cambridge.

It furthers the University's mission by disseminating knowledge in the pursuit of
education, learning and research at the highest international levels of excellence.

www.cambridge.org
Information on this title: www.cambridge.org/9781107643161

© Cambridge University Press 1906

First published 1906
Re-issued 2014

A catalogue record for this publication is available from the British Library

ISBN 978-1-107-64316-1 Paperback

PREFACE.

IN November 1905, the Bishop of Lincoln did me the honour to pass on to me a question about the official position of certain English Prelates of the Southern Province in the Episcopal College ; an enquiry in which the Bishop of Bristol was interested at the time.

Recollecting that Archbishop Benson had long ago written to me on a kindred subject, I looked up his letter, and such notes as I have preserved indicating the grounds of my reply to him.

The present Primate of all England (hearing, as it appears, that I had been writing upon the subject) in very kind terms has suggested that I should put the result on record.

I have thought accordingly, that I could best comply with his Grace's desire by offering the following notes in print to the consideration of such readers as may care to examine them.

It remains for me to express my thanks to the Reverend Edward S. Dewick, F.S.A., Dr J. Wickham Legg, F.S.A., Leopold G. Wickham Legg, Esq., M.A., and Arthur Russell Malden, Esq., M.A., for their kind help while these pages were passing through the Press : as well as to Mr John Clay and his assistants at Cambridge.

CHR. W.

ST PETER'S RECTORY,
MARLBOROUGH.

ʼΑπόδοτε πᾶϲιν τὰϲ ὀφειλάϲ,
...τῶι τὴν τιμὴν τὴν τιμήν.

Ad Rom. xiii. 7.

CONTENTS.

Contents

Contents

INTRODUCTORY NOTE.

A reference to the fact that the Bishop of London held the position of Dean among the English Bishops as early as 1162[1] suggests the idea that the origin of a PROVINCIAL CHAPTER consisting of members of the COLLEGE OF BISHOPS is of remote antiquity.

Whether or not it was an institution imported from Normandy or elsewhere we are unable to determine.

An attempt is made in the following pamphlet to ascertain the office and position of certain Bishops in the Provincial Chapter of Canterbury, and likewise to trace the history of the Precedence of certain English Prelates.

The following letter, addressed by the late Archbishop Benson to the writer, is printed as introductory to the two-fold enquiry.

[1] See Appendix (*B***), p. 81, below.

I. Dr E. W. Benson, Archbishop of Canterbury, to the Rev. Chr. Wordsworth, M.A.

ADDINGTON PARK, CROYDON.
27 *Nov.*, 1886.

My dear Christopher W.,

Would you look at these papers for me? I have entertained a contrary opinion, but I am disposed to think the points of apparent difference really mean that the Bishop of Winton was Chancellor, but that in the vacancy of the See of London he acted as Bishop of London (Dean) should have acted, and was called for the time Subdean.

That he was Subdean in the vacancy only—and Lincoln Vice-Chancellor ordinarily, but Chancellor in the vacancy of Winton.

Still I am not sure that this is exactly compatible with the extract from Arundel.

It would be very strange if such a usage had got out of gear, or [had] been altered between Arundel and Parker.—Would it not?

I shall be so grateful for your investigation and opinion. I do not know whether anything else can be made out or discovered in the Library.

Your ever affectionate

EDV. CANTUAR.

[The question had been put to the Archbishop by Dr E. Harold Browne, Bishop of Winchester, in a letter dated "Farnham Castle, Surrey, Nov. 16, 1886." The letter is not forthcoming; but I gather from notes which I made at the time that the Bishop of Winton was of opinion that, in consequence of the προεδρία of London and Winton, the offices of Dean and Subdean (or Chancellor) were given them in the Provincial Chapter; that the capitular prelates (Sarum, Lincoln, Worcester and Rochester) gained no fresh precedence. At one period, Winton, as Prelate of the Garter[1], took precedence of *all* bishops, and thus became Dean of the Chapel Royal.

But 31 Hen. VIII. (1539), cap. 10 § 3, orders that the King's Vicegerent shall sit on the form

---

[1] The order of the Garter was instituted in, or before, 1347.

K. Edward III., its founder, established as its principal officer a *Prelate*, under whom were a *Registrar* and an *Usher*. At a later date, a second principal officer, the *Chancellor*, was added; and likewise *Garter*, as one of the subordinate or inferior officers of the Order. All five are sworn of the Council of the Order.

William of Edyngdon and his successors as Bishops of Winchester from the first foundation of the order have held the office of *Prelate* of the Garter, as Earls of Southampton, according to the Statutes of the Order:—"Quisquis autem presul Wintoniensis ac Southamtonie comes *et cet.* eo tempore fuerit, is et Prelatus ordinis esse debet." (Statut. Lib. N. p. 232, art. 18, ap. El. Ashmole, *Appendix to History of the Garter*, fo. 1672, p. 34; id. *Hist.* p. 234, S. H. Cassan, *Lives of Bishops of Winchester*, ii. 289—93.)

The *Chancellorship* of the Order of the Garter was conferred on Bishops of Salisbury from 1475 to 1535, and after being held for 150 years by laymen, it was restored to Sarum under a royal decree of 19 Nov. 1669, to take effect at the next vacancy. When Berks (and Windsor with it) was transferred to Oxford in 1836 the Chancellorship of the Order was allowed to the Bishops of Oxford. (W. H. Jones, *Fasti Eccl. Sarisb.* 1879, p. 61.)

to the right of the Throne with the Archbishop, who shall sit next; then, York, London, *Durham*, Winton, &c.

Bishop E. H. Browne thought that this Act of King Henry VIII. was the first to give Durham precedence of Winchester, and that while its authority is of general application as to precedence in other cases, it does not over-rule the Canon as to a seat in Synod, which in terms suited to his invariable sweetness of manner he claimed for his see in cases where Anglican prelates might be assembled synodically[1].

Three or four of the following extracts were submitted by the then Bishop of Winchester, the remainder were forwarded by me to the Primate in 1886. I have now brought them so far up to date, as I have been able.]

II. WILLIAM OF MALMESBURY.

[*De Concilio Regni*, A.D. 1072 *habito.*]

HABEBAT autem ex antiquo, sicut in libro primo dixisse me memini[2], Cantuariensis archiepiscopus hos episcopos:—

Londoniensem, Wintoniensem, Rofensem, Scire-

---

[1] The third Lambeth Conference, or Pan-Anglican Synod was within measurable distance at the time, meeting, as it did, in July, 1888. I well remember the *jucunda senectus* of Bishop Browne of Winchester, who had ordained me deacon when he was at Ely. It was at an earlier period in his life when Dr Jacobson, an Oxonian Professor and Bishop of Chester, exclaimed after making his first acquaintance with his Cambridge equal, "I have often heard of 'the *milk* of human kindness'; but now I've seen the *cow*!"

[2] Will. Malmesb. *De Gestis Regum* i. § 99—103, Rolls Series, i. pp. 100, 101.

burnensem, Wigornensem, Herefordensem, Lichet-
feldensem, Selesiensem, Legacestrensem, Elmanen-
sem, Sidnacestrensem, Domuccensem : additi sunt,
tempore regis Edwardi senioris[1], Cornubiensis,
Cridiensis, Wellensis in West-Saxonia, et in Merciis
Dorcestrensis, ut secundo libro dixi[2].

Eboracensis autem archiepiscopus habebat omnes
trans Humbram episcopos suæ ditioni subjectos,

Ripensem, Haugustaldensem, Lindisfarnensem,
illum de Candida Casa quæ nunc Witerne dicitur, et
omnes episcopos Scotiæ et Orcadum ;

sicut Cantuariensis habet episcopos Hiberniæ et
Walarum.

Perierunt autem jamdudum episcopatus Ripensis
et Haugustaldensis vi hostilitatis ; et Legacestrensis,
et Sidnacestrensis et Dommuccensis, quo nescio
modo.

Porro autem tempore regis Edwardi simplicis[3],
Cornubiensis et Cridiensis uniti sunt, et translatus
est episcopatus in Exoniam.

Sub rege Willelmo, in isto eodem concilio pro-
nuntiatum est, secundum scita canonum, ut episcopi
transeuntes de villis constituerent [*al.* 'construerent']
sedes suas in urbibus diocesium suarum : Licitfeldensis ergo migravit [*al.* 'transiit'] in Cestram,
quæ olim Civitatis Legionum dicebatur ; Selesiensis
in Cicestram ; Elmanensis in Tethford primo, nunc
ab Herberto episcopo in Norwic ; Scirburnensis in
Salisbiriam ; Dorcestrensis in Lincoliam.   Nam

---

[1] Edward the Elder, son of Alfred: cf. *Gesta Regum* ii. § 129,
vol. I. 140—1, from Leofric Missal, fo. 1.

[2] *Gesta Regum* ii. § 129; Rolls S. i. p. 141.

[3] *i.e.* Edward Confessor.   Cf. § 196; II. p. 236.

Lindisfarnensis pridem veteri tempore transierat in Dunelmum, et nuper Wellensis in Bathoniam.

(*Gesta Regum*, lib. iii. § 300, vol. ii. pp. 352–3.)

[*De* proëdria *singulorum episcoporum in concilio.*]

IN hoc conventu Lanfrancus, qui erat adhuc rudis Anglus, quæsivit a senioribus episcopis qui esset ordo sedendi in concilio, antiquo more statutus : illi vero, excusata difficultate responsi, in diem distulerunt posterum. Et tunc, diligentissime advocata memoria, hunc se vidisse morem asseruere ; ut Cantuariæ archiepiscopus, concilio præsidens, habeat

> a dextro latere archiepiscopum Eboraci, et
> juxta eum episcopum Wintoniæ,
> a sinistro autem Londoniensem :

quod si, ut contingit, pro aliqua necessitate Cantuariensis primas adventum suum negaverit [*al.* 'excusaverit'], vel obitu defuerit, Eboracensis archiepiscopus, concilio præsidens, habeat

> a dextra Londoniensem episcopum,
> a sinistra Wintoniensem ;

ceteri secundum tempora ordinationum, sedilia sua agnoscant. (*Gesta Regum* iii. § 301 ; vol. ii. p. 353.)

[York had claimed Worcester and Dorchester as suffragans, but the pope having referred the dispute to the English Council, it was after much discussion then agreed (at Windsor, in 1072) "ut quia citra Humbram essent, hi episcopi Cantuariensi

applicarentur, omnes vero Transhumbranos Eboracensis obtineret." (§ 302; ii. p. 354.)]

[If we may judge from the order of signatures
of Bishops, &c. at the Council of Windsor in 1072,
Winchester had not then acquired this precedence
which was to be determined in the following year.

The order of signatures in 1072 had been:—
1. King; 2. Queen; 3. Legate; 4. Canterbury;
5. York; 6. London; 7. Sherborne (Sarum);
8. Worcester; 9. Hereford; 10. Wells; 11. Dorchester (Lincoln); 12. Winchester; 13. Elmham
(Norwich); 14. Chichester; 15. Rochester; 16.
Exeter; 17. Bayeux; 18. Coutances.

(Wilkins, *Concilia* i. 325.)

Gervase of Canterbury (*Acta Pontificum*, col.
1654, cited by Wilkins, *Conc.* i. 369) in his account
of the Council of London under Lanfranc, omits all
mention of any special priority for Winchester.]

III.   COUNCIL OF LONDON, 9 Will. I. (1075).

Concilium Londini celebratum A.D. 1075, præsidente
Lanfranco Dorobernensis ecclesiæ archipræsule.

ANNO incarnationis Dominicæ .Mlxxv. regnante
[glorioso Anglorum rege] Willielmo, anno [regni
eius] ix°., congregatum est in Lundonia [in ecclesia
beati Pauli apostoli] concilium [totius Angliæ regio-
nis, episcoporum videlicet et abbatum, necnon et
multarum religiosi ordinis personarum, jubente, atque
eidem concilio] præsidente, Lanfranco archiepiscopo
[sanctæ] Dorobernensi[s ecclesiæ archipræsule, totius-
que Britanniæ insulæ primate]

considentibus secum [viris venerabilibus]
Thoma Eboracensi archiepiscopo
Willielmo Londoniensi episcopo
† Goisfrido Constantiensi[1], qui cum transmarinus esset episcopus in Anglia multas possessiones habens cum ceteris in concilio residebat †
Walkelino Wintoniensi
Hermanno Siraburnensi
Wlstano Wiricestrensi
Walter(i)o Herefordensi
Gisone Wellensi
Remigio Dor(ca)censi, seu Lincoliensi
Herfasto Helmeanensi, sive Nor(ch)wicensi
Stigando Seleugensi (*al.* Selengensi)[2]
Osberno Exoniensi
Petro Licedfeldensi (*al.* Licitfeldensi);

Rof(f)ensis ecclesia per id[em] tempus pastore carebat; Lindisfarnensis (qui et Dunelmensis) episcopus, canonicam excusationem habens, concilio interesse non poterat [*al.* 'potuit'].

Et quia multis retro annis in Anglico regno usus conciliorum obsoleverat, renovata sunt nonnulla quæ

---

[1] Geoffrey de Montbray, who became bishop of Coutances in 1048, presided as Chief Justiciar in 1071. He came over with William, and acted as interpreter at his coronation in 1066. He held (*e.g.*) in Wilts the manors of Draycot Cerne, Withenham and Winfield in Bradford hundred, Malmesbury, Pertwood, Littleton Drew, and Winterbourn (? Dauntsey). W. H. Jones, *Wilts Domesday*, 26—7. Geoffrey headed the rising of barons against William II., by whom he was pardoned. He maintained the privileges of the clergy, at Salisbury, in 1088.

†—† Geoffrey of Coutances is passed over in MSS. of *Gesta Pontificum* in this connexion.

[2] It will be observed that *after* the council, Stigand subscribes the resolutions or canons as 'Cicestrensis.' (Wilkins *Concil.* i. 373—4.)

antiquis etiam canonibus noscuntur [*al.* 'fuerant,' *al.* 'sunt diffinitionibus '] definita [*al.* 'diffinita ']. Ex concilio igitur Toletano IV. [a°. 633][1], Milevitano [a°. 402][2] atque Brac*h*arensi [a°. 599][3] statutum est, vt

Singuli secundum ordinationis suæ tempora sedeant, præter eos qui ex antiqua consuetudine, sive suarum æcclesiarum privilegiis, digniores sedes habent.

De qua re interrogati sunt senes et ætate provecti, quid vel ipsi vidissent, vel a majoribus atque antiquioribus veraciter ac probabiliter [ipsi] accepissent [*al.* 'audissent,' *vel* 'vidissent ']. Super quo responso petitæ sunt indutiæ, ac concessæ, usque in crastinum.

Crastina autem die, concorditer perhibuere, quod

Eboracensis archiepiscopus ad dexteram Dorobernensis sedere debeat ;

Lundoniensis episcopus ad sinistram ;

Wentanus, juxta Eboracensem.

Si vero Eboracensis desit,

Lundoniensis, ad dexteram,

Wentanus, ad sinistram.

(*After some regulations respecting monasteries*)

Ex decretis summorum pontificum, Damasi [videlicet,] et Leonis, necnon ex conciliis Sardicensi (a°. 347)[4] atque Laodicensi (a°. 366)[5] in quibus

---

[1] 'Omnes episcopi pariter introeant, et secundum ordinationis suæ tempus (*al.* 'tempora') resideant.' *Concil. Tolet.* IV. c. 4, ed. Bruns, i. 222.

[2] Cf. *Codex Eccl. Africanæ* cc. lxxxvi., lxxxix., ed. Bruns, 177—8.

[3] Cf. *Concil. Bracar.* c. 34, Bruns, ii. p. 34.

[4] Cf. *Concil. Sardic.* c. 1, ed. Bruns, i. p. 88 (89).

[5] *Concil. Laodiceni* c. 57, Bruns, i. 79.

prohibetur episcopales sedes in villis existere, concessum est regia munificentia et synodali auctoritate [præfatis tribus] episcopis de villis ad civitates transire[1] :

Herimanno, de Siraburna [*al.* 'Schireburne'] ad Serisberiam [*al.* 'Sarisberiam,' *vel* 'Salisberiam']

Stigando, de Selengeo [*al.* 'Selesia'] ad Cicestr(i)am [*al.* 'Cicestrum']

Petro, de Licitfelde [*al.* 'Licefelda,' *vel* 'Lichfeld'] ad Cestr(i)am [*al.* 'Cestrum'].

[De quibusdam, qui in villis seu vicis adhuc degebant, dilatum est usque ad regis audientiam, qui in transmarinis partibus tunc temporis bella gerebat.][2]

(After 6 other canons, the subscriptions of prelates follow :—)

Date of Consecration	
1070 Aug. 29	✠ Ego Lanfrancus Dorobernensis archiep. subscripsi.
1070	✠ Ego Thomas Eboracensis ecclesiæ episc. subscr.
1051	✠ Ego Willielmus Lundoniensis eccl. ep. subscr.
1070 May 30	✠ Ego Walkelinus Wintoniensis eccl. ep. subscr.
[1048]	✠ Ego Gauffridus Constantiensis ep., et unus de Angliæ terræ primatibus subscr.[3]
1045	✠ Ego Hermannus Sarisberiensis ['Siraburnensis'] eccl. ep. subscr.

[1] See p. 4, above.

[2] Lincoln cathedral was begun cir. 1074 ; foundation charter, Sept. 1090. Consecration, 1092. See of Wells removed to Bath, 1088.

[3] The name of the Norman bishop of Coutances appears between London and Winton in the previous list of prelates present at the Synod. But in subscribing the acts after precedence was determined he takes a position *after* the four more honourable English sees.

Date of
Conse-
cration

1062 Sep. 8	✠ Ego Wlstanus Wigornensis ['Wircustrensis'] ep. subscr.[1]
1061	✠ Ego Walterus Herefordensis ep. subscr.
1061	✠ Ego Giso Wellensis ep. subscr.
1067	✠ Ego Remigius Lincol(n)iensis ep. subscr.
1070	✠ Ego Herfastus Norhwicensis ep. subscr.
1070	✠ Ego Stigandus Cicestrensis ep. subscr.
1072	✠ Ego Osbernus Exoniensis ep. subscr.
1072	✠ Ego Petrus Cestrensis episcopus subscripsi.

Then follow the signatures of Aschenil, Anschitil, or Anschibil, archdeacon of Canterbury ('Doroberniensis eccl.') *and* 21 abbots.

[The preceding account of the Council of London in 1075 is extracted from Spelman's printing of the Worcester MS. register in his *Concilia* ii. 7—9. Cf. Wilkins, *Concil.* i. 373-4. I have inserted in brackets some various readings from Spelman's print of another exemplar from W. of Malmesbury and Bigne, iii. 1280. Spelman, *Concil.* ii. 9, 10; Wilkins, *Concil.* i. 374. This I have again compared with Malmesbury's *Gesta Pontificum* i. ff. 22^b —23^b. Rolls Series, pp. 66—8.

The *signatures* of those present in this Council are not given (according to Spelman) except in the Worcester Register. The *list* of those present is found in the same authority. Spelman's third exemplar, a 12th century MS. in Cambridge Univ. Library (Ff. i. 25), names only the two archbishops, and the bishops of *London* and *Worcester* (passing

---

[1] It seems that the Bishop of Worcester placed himself before two of his seniors by consecration. Or are we to suspect the scribe of the Worcester MS. of partiality in transcribing the record?

over Coutances, Winchester, and Sherborne or Sarum), and giving the numbers as the two archbishops and two bishops already named "cum aliis .xj." which gives a total of one more than we can account for. Spelman's other authority, viz. W. of Malmesbury's *Gesta Pontificum*, lib. i. p. 66, does not give the list of those present or the signatories in the earliest texts. The list however (as the Rolls editor, N. E. S. A. Hamilton, shows) was added in MS. *A* (Magd. Coll. Oxon. 172) over an erasure, and partly in the lower margin; but it seems to have incorporated these from the earlier text of the 12th century MSS. *B* and *C* (Brit. Mus. Cotton Claud. A. 5; Harl. 364) which contain the list. From the years of consecration, which we have added in the margin, it will be seen that after a few specially privileged sees the names follow pretty closely the order of consecration. Rochester, being vacant, by the death of Siward, who held that bishopric 1058—75, is of course not represented at this Council held in 1075. All the bishops were present, with the exception of Walcher of Durham, who had 'a canonical excuse.' At the time of the earlier Council in 1072 the bishop of Durham, Ethelwin, was expelled from his see in 1071 and imprisoned[1]. He was succeeded in 1071 by Walcher; consecrated in March. It was, I believe, in 1072, that Durham was declared to belong to the province of York, for which Lincoln (or Dorchester), Worcester and Lichfield had been also claimed as suffragans[2].

---

[1] Roger Wendover ad ann. 1071.
[2] Cf. *Gesta Pontif.* 41, 285.

The Cambridge MS., cited by Spelman, *Concil.* ii. 10, 11 (in Dugdale's *St Paul's*, ed. 1818, p. 302), has the following addition, under the date 1075, but according to W. of Malmesbury it belonged rather to the year 1072 :—]

IN illis temporibus diversis auctoritatibus[1] probatum atque ostensum est, quod Eboracensis æcclesia Cantuariensi æcclesiæ debeat subjacere, ejusque archiepiscopi ut primatis totius Britanniæ dispositionibus, in hiis quæ ad Christianam religionem pertinent, in omnibus obedire.

Subjectionem vero Dunelmensis [hoc est Lindisfarnensis] episcopi atque terminos a fluvio Humbre usque ad ultimos fines Scottiæ, sub regimine Eboracensis æcclesiæ affirmaverunt[2]:

professionem cum sacramento vero, ob amorem regis, Thomæ Eboracensi archiepiscopo Lanfrancus archiepiscopus relaxavit ; scriptamque tantum professionem recepit, non præjudicans successoribus suis, qui sacramentum cum professione a successoribus Thomæ exigere voluerint.

(*W. of Malmesbury adds:*—)

Si archiepiscopus Cantuariensis vitam finierit, Eboracensis archiepiscopus Doroberniam veniet ; et

---

[1] The passage occurs almost verbatim in *Gesta Pontificum,* pp. 42—3, under the date 1072 among the reasons ascribed to Thomas, Abp of York, "Et tandem aliquando diversis diversarum causarum auctoritatibus..."

[2] 'Subjectionem vero Dunelmensis (hoc est Lindisfarnensis) episcopi atque omnium regionum a terminis Licitfeldensis episcopii † et Humbræ magni fluvii usque ad extremos Scottiæ fines, et quicquid ex hac parte prædicti fluminis ad parrochiam Eboracensis æcclesiæ jure competit, Cantuariensis metropolitanus Eboracensi archiepiscopo ejusque successoribus in perpetuum obtinere concessit.' *Gesta Pontificum* (s.a. 1072), p. 43.   † *Sic.*

eum qui electus fuerit cum ceteris præfatæ æcclesiæ episcopis, ut primatem proprium jure consecrabit.

Quod si archiepiscopus Eboracensis obierit, is qui ei successurus eligitur accepto a rege archiepiscopatus dono[1], Cantuariam, vel ubi Cantuariensi archiepiscopo visum fuerit accedet, et ab ipso ordinationem canonico more suscipiet.

(*Gesta Pontificum*, pp. 42, 43.)

[In 1114, Ralph d'Escures, Archbishop of Canterbury, refused to consecrate Thurstan to the Archbishopric of York, until he promised canonical obedience to the see of Canterbury.]

[Roger, Bishop of Salisbury (1107–39), the King's Chancellor, was consecrated by Abp Anselm, having

---

[1] *Accepto a rege archiepiscopatus dono*: Students of Church History will not need to be reminded that the claims of the Crown in episcopal promotions are not entirely an invention of Tudor policy. The following letter was written by Archbishop Temple to my Brother, the Bishop of Salisbury:—

25 *Dec.* 1896.

The *Confirmation* of a Bishop or Archbishop.

"Whatever the Court may once have been, it is, I have little doubt, on precisely the same footing as the *congé d'élire*: as dead, and as living. Its purpose now is to certify the Queen that all the proceedings have been according to law. If in any case the Dean and Chapter were to elect the wrong man (which might conceivably have been done in the Hampden case, for —— was half cracked) it would be the duty of the Court, instead of confirming, to report adversely to the Queen. Or if it could be said that the Chapter had not been rightly summoned, some one having been left out, who had a right to be there, it would be the duty of the Court to hear such an objection.

I do not believe that the Court was ever a Court of Heresy at any time. The Court however is properly the Court of the Archbishop, and I shall certainly look into it before long.

Yours ever,

F. CANTUAR."

refused consecration at the hands of Girard, Abp of York.

In 1121 K. Henry I. was married to Adelis of Lorraine at Windsor. The Bishop of Salisbury asserted his right to celebrate the royal espousals, but was refused.]

IV. W. OF MALMESBURY, *Gesta Pontificum* ex codd. MSS. (prioris recensionis) Cotton. et Harl.

Cum rex Henricus, defuncta priore conjuge Mathildi, Adelidem puellam filiam ducis Lotharingorum ducere intendisset, sponsalia apud Windlesoras fieri placuit.

Id officium Rogerius Salesberiensis episcopus sibi deberi dixit, quod [pro] titubantia linguae archiepiscopus explere nequiret, et quod sua diocesis esset.

Restitit ille homini tum maxime potenti, adeo ut jam sacris vestibus indutum episcopum exuviis cedere cogeret: tum quia ipse inequalis erat, Willelmo Wentano [episcopo] hoc delegavit muneris, caute[lae] inposterum providens, ne quid tale Salesberiensis episcopus pro privilegio parrochiae sibi assumeret....

(Gesta Pontificum, p. 132 *n.*)

§ 72. *De Episcopis Rofæ.*—Cantuariensem aecclesiam sequitur Rofensis, vicinitate loci non auctoritate privilegii proxima[1]. (*ibid.* p. 133.)

[Abp Parker, in *De Antiquitate Ecclesiæ Britannicæ* (p. 24 = 31), quotes a letter of John of Pontoise, Bishop of Winchester, written in "1284" [? 1303],

---

[1] A disclaimer from Rochester, sent to Salisbury in 1221, will be given below.

acting as Subdean in the vacancy of the see of London, which lasted for three years. It will be observed that the Bp of Winchester here modestly subscribes himself "Your Grace's Chaplain," somewhat as Dr Benson used in writing to my Father to style himself, "Your...bedesman."]

V. EPISTOLA JOHANNIS [DE PONTISSARA] WINTONIENSIS [EPISCOPI]: ad...[1] Cantuariensem Archiepiscopum. [Mense Decembri A.D. 1303.]

REVERENDISSIMO in Christo patri et domino charissimo, suus devotus Capellanus, quicquid potest obedientiæ reverentiæ et honoris.

Præeminenciæ vestræ litteras per harum bajulum nobis missas recepimus .xj. die Decembris, quæ mixturam quandam doloris et gaudii continebant: Iniicit nimirum animo nostro mæstitiam, quod hominem gratum Deo, justum, mansuetum et pium, et his diebus malis regno Angliæ tum necessarium, bonæ memoriæ dñm Richardum Londini episcopum ab hac luce mors amara subtraxit, sed materiam quandam gaudii et consolationis subministrat, quod excellentiam vestram, ad nostra et Ecclesiæ nostræ Wintoniensis jura conservanda et augenda literarum earundem relatu cognovimus, quadam spiritualis

x Flori-io.][2]

---

[1] Abp Parker here prints (*ad*) *Johannem Peckham*, as the name of his predecessor. But the reference is to the decease of Richard de Gravesend Bp of London, which occurred 9 Dec. 1303, and seems to have been mentioned by the Archbishop in his letter to the Bp of Winton two days later, and to have been noticed in the reply sent back by the hand of the bearer of the news, probably with some promptitude. The letter, therefore, must belong to the primacy of *Robert Winchelsey*, who had succeeded on Peckham's death in 1294.

[2] '*Ex archĕtycho* [*sic*]. Anno 1284.' Parker *Antiq. Brit.* ed. 1605, p. 21, *margin*.

dilectionis prærogativa sollicitam et internam, pro quo vestræ dignationi grates, licet exiles et tantis meritis impares, quantas pro tempore possumus, exhibemus. Ex hoc nempe laudis et honoris titulum vestra præcellens dignitas promeretur, quæ tamen se reputat honoratam, cum, qui singulis quibusque debetur fratribus, honor debitus non negatur. Ait enim beatus Gregorius : *meus honor est fratrum meorum solidus vigor.* Verum, quia alibi scribitur, temporis indigemus, ut aliquid maturius agamus, ne præcipitemus concilia et opera nostra, neque eorum ordinem corrumpamus, deliberationem nostram super hoc fecimus. Quod ejus vices, eo mortuo vel absente, gerere et exequi ad nos tanquam ad vestrorum suffraganeorum Subdecanum iure consuetudinario dictas pertinere, consultis nostris dilectis filiis, Priore et Capitulo nostro Winton : cum omni celeritate accommoda absque moræ dispendio rescribemus ; firmum semper habentes propositum et promptum gerentes animum ad vestra præcepta et beneplacita exequenda. Incolumitatem vestram in longa tempora protendat Altissimus ad regimen Ecclesiæ sponsæ suæ. Scriptum apud Farnham die prædicto.

Capellanus vester Wintoniensis.

(M. Parker, *De Antiquitate Eccl. Brit.*

1572, p. 24 = 21, ed. 1605).

[For some other notes relating to the period 1303–13, see no. IX. below. The following document from Lambeth contains further information.]

VI. REGISTER OF THOMAS ARUNDEL,
Abp of Canterbury, A.D. 1404.

Convocatio Prelatorum et Cleri Cantuariensis
provincie. 24 Nov. 1404.

DICTO die 24° mensis Novembris, missa de sancto
Spiritu ad summum altare ipsius cathedralis ecclesie
more solito solempniter celebrata, et deinde facta
collatione in capella beate Marie ejusdem ecclesie,
coram eodem reverendissimo patre et suis suffraganeis ac aliis prelatis et clero dicte sue Cantuariensis
provincie tunc ibidem presentibus, et lecto deinceps
certificatorio venerabilis patris domini Henrici, Dei
gracia Lincolniensis episcopi, de et super convoca-
cione huiusmodi, cujus tenor sequitur in hec verba :—

*Certificatorium Episcopi Lincoln., sedibus
London et Winton vacantibus.*

REVERENDISSIMO in Christo patri et domino
domino Thome, Dei gracia Cantuariensi archiepiscopo, tocius Anglie primati et apostolice sedis
legato, Henricus permissione divina Lincolniensis
episcopus, obedienciam, reverenciam et honorem
tanto patri debitas cum omnimoda subjeccione tam
debita quam devota.

Mandatum vestrum reverendum nobis .xxiij. die
mensis Octobris ultimo jam predicti literatim cum
ea qua decuit reverencia recepimus in hec verba :

THOMAS permissione divina Cantuariensis archiepiscopus tocius Anglie primas, et apostolice sedis
legatus, venerabili fratri nostro domino Henrico Dei
gracia Lincolnien. episcopo, qui tanquam sacrosancte

nostre Cantuariensis ecclesie Cancellarius, vacantibus Londoniensi et Winton. ecclesiis, que ipsius ecclesie nostre Cantuariensis Decanatus et Subdecanatus decorantur munere (*al.* 'numero') et honore, mandata nostra et ipsius ecclesie ex debito vestri officii recipere et exequi tenemini cum effectu Salutem et fraternam in Domino caritatem, *&c.*

(*Ex Registro* T. Arundel *archiepisc.* fo. 62[b].)

[An authoritative statement is given in 1433, in the *Provinciale* of W. Lyndwood, Dean of Arches and Keeper of the Privy Seal, and subsequently Bishop of St David's, 1442–6. Lyndwood had been connected with Salisbury (as prebendary of Ruscomb, 1412–24, and of Bishopston, 1424–34) and subsequently with Lincoln, as Archdeacon of Oxford in 1438, and of Stow in June, 1439.—In the text, Abp H. Chichele's Constitution, 17 Dec. 1416, prescribes that the Feast of St John of Beverley should be observed on May 7th, "cum regimine chori *secundum usum* Sarum *ecclesiæ*," whereon he glosses :—]

VII.   W. Lyndwood, LL.D., Dean of Arches, Archdeacon of Oxford. In *Provinciali* seu *Constitutionibus Angliæ*, 1433.

Usum Sarum Ecclesiae. > Opponitur contra hoc, 12. distinct. *de his.* ubi ordinatur, quod officium divinum servari debet, et dici per totam provinciam, secundum modum et usum metropolitanæ ecclesiæ, et concordat ad hoc *De Consecratione.* distinct. 1. 'Altaria,' et distinct. 2. 'Institutio.'[1]

Solutio.   Dic, quod hoc, quod allegatur pro contrario, verum est a parte Juris Communis ; illud

---

[1] Decreti III. Pars, dist. i. cap. 31 ; dist. ii. cap. 31.

tamen, quod hic dicitur, *de usu Sarum tenendo*, ortum habet ex longa consuetudine, quæ, cum sit rationabilis, tenenda est. Sic sentit Archid.[1] d. c. 'Altaria.' Et notatur *De officio ordinarii* § 'Quod pertinet,' sub § 'Sunt autem,' vers. 'varium': per Hostiensem[2] in *Summa* et *De supplenda negligentia prælatorum,* c. 1, per Cardinalem[3] vers. 'Concessum,' vers. 'Officium varium,' lib. 6.—Vel dic, quod ad solutionem contrarii sufficit, sic fore hic statutum, maxime cum quasi tota provincia hunc usum sequatur. Facit *Instit.* 'De usucapionibus § *'Furtivæ'* et *Instit.* '*Qui, et ex quibus causis manumittere non possunt,*' in principio. ff.[4] '*Qui, et a quibus.*' in lege 'Prospexit.'

Episcopus namque Sarum in collegio episcoporum est Præcentor, et temporibus quibus Archiepiscopus Cantuariensis solenniter celebrat divina, præsente collegio episcoporum, chorum in divinis officiis regere debet de observantia et consuetudine antiqua.

> *Provinciale,* lib. ii. tit. 3 ('Anglicanæ Ecclesiæ.' Et infra, 'Statuimus igitur... *secundum usum Sarum Ecclesiæ* per provinciam nostram antedictam futuris temporibus perpetuo celebretur'). Ed. *Oxon.* fol. 1679, 1. 104, *gloss.*

---

[1] *Archid. i.e.* Guido Baifius, Archdeacon of Bologna, who flourished cir. 1300, in his Commentary on the Decretum of Gratian.

[2] *Hostiensis, i.e.* Cardinal Henricus de Segusia of Ostia. *Summa Aurea,* bk. 1, col. 134, ed. Basil, 1573.

[3] *Cardinal, i.e.* Francis de Zabarellis of Padua, cir. 1410.

[4] "ff." a corruption of Π=Pandectes, thus stands for *Digestum.* '*Furtivæ'*=Justiniani *Institutiones* II. tit. vi. § 2. 'Qui, et ex quibus causis'=*Instit.* I. tit. vi. '*Qui, et a quibus*'=*Digest.* XL. tit. ix., where lex 12 begins "Prospexit legislator" (Ulpian, lib. v. *de Adulteriis*).

[Another passage, later in the *Provinciale*, with its gloss, has some bearing on our subject. Abp Boniface, in the first of the Constitutions issued at Lambeth in 1261 (Friday, May 13), decrees that in case the King summons them to answer in a secular court concerning their ecclesiastical office, the prelates shall resent such infringement of their liberties, and, if he persists, shall lay their dioceses under an interdict. They must refuse to show the acts of ecclesiastical courts in a secular court, although any party to an ecclesiastical suit may peruse them (*Constit. Othon.* 29, A.D. 1237). The conclusion of this lengthy Constitution of Boniface is as follows :—]

VIII.   Constitutions of Lambeth, under Abp Boniface, 1261.

Et si clericus fuerit, qui propter hoc fuerit arrestatus, diœcesanus taliter arrestati vel impetiti clerici, vel Archiepiscopus, aut Episcopus Londinensis tanquam Episcoporum Decanus, cum aliquibus episcopis sibi associatis, sicut si fuerit episcopus arrestatus requirat eum, et puniat[1] detentores. Et si necesse fuerit in hoc casu procedatur ad pœnas superius annotatas.

(*Glossa*) 𝕰𝖕𝖎𝖘𝖈𝖔𝖕𝖚𝖘 𝕷𝖔𝖓𝖉𝖎𝖓𝖊𝖓𝖘𝖎𝖘. > Quando archiepiscopus est absens.

> W. Lyndwood, *Provinciale*, Lib. v. tit. 15 *Æternæ sanctio voluntatis*, et infra, *cum sæpe contingat...Et si clericus.*   Ed. Oxon. 1679, i. p. 318; cf. iii. 17.

[1] 'puniant': *in printed text; but* 'puniat', *in gloss*, i. 318.

[Earlier in the same 1st Constitution there is a passage, more explicit, where it treats of prelates expostulating with the King :—]

Et si [Rex] non destiterit, tunc, ad denunciationem episcopi, Archiepiscopus, convocatis duobus episcopis, vel tribus, vel pluribus, quos duxerit evocandos, si in provincia extiterent : alioquin Londinensis Episcopus tanquam Episcoporum Decanus, duobus Episcopis vel pluribus sibi adjunctis, dominum Regem adeant, et ipsum moneant, diligentius requirentes quod mandatis supersedeat supradictis, *&c.*

(*Glossa*) **Alioquin.** > Scilicet, si fuerit [Archiepiscopus] extra provinciam.

Tanquam > Vere ponitur, et non`similitudinarie. Habet[1] namque Archiepiscopus Cantuariensis in Collegio Episcoporum Episcopos,

Londoniensem, Decanum,
Wintoniensem, Cancellarium,
Lincolniensem, Vicecancellarium,
Sarisburiensem, Præcentorem,
Wigorniensem, Capellanum,
Roffensem, Cruciferarium.

Provinciale, Lib. v. tit. 15, *De Pœnis*. Ed. Oxon. i. pp. 316, 317; cf. id. iii. p. 16. Cf. J. Johnson, *Canons*, ed. 1851, pp. 188, 189 ; Spelman, *Concilia*, ii. 307 ; Wilkins, *Concilia*, i. 746 foll. Gibson, *Codex*, ed. 1761, ii. 1021.

---

[1] The following lines are cited in MS. Lambeth, 751, fol. 7. See No. ix. (8) below.

IX. With Lyndwood agrees the old *Forma sive Descriptio Convocationis celebrandæ,* of which there is a later transcript among Abp Tenison's MSS. in the Library of Lambeth Palace, cod. 751.

Though comparatively modern, its contents are interesting, and I accordingly append a summary supplied me by Miss E. Margaret Thompson, and partly from my own notes, while citing the passages which concern our present enquiry.

Lambeth MS. 751.

(1) Forma sive descriptio convocationis cele-brande, prout ab antiquo observari consuevit. lf. 1—4ᵇ.

(2) Forma eligendi et presentandi prolocutorem. lf. 5—7.

[These opening sections were twice printed about 1700–2¹, probably under the editorship of Edmund Gibson the Canonist (afterwards Bp of Lincoln and subsequently of London), who at that time was chaplain and librarian to Abp Tenison.]

(3) A Note out of an old Recorde.

These things that follow be necessarilie requisite in time of Consecration of a Busshope

---

¹ First, *Forma sive Descriptio Convocationis Celebrandæ,* pp. 1—12, without date or editor's name. A copy is at Lambeth (77 A. 4) and another in the British Museum. Second, in the middle of [Edmund Gibson's] *Synodus Anglicana* 8vo. ed. 2 [1702], where these sections occupy pp. 1—6 of the new pagination which comes between p. 222 (blank) and *recto* 175: *verso* 222 (*bis*), so that the catchword is twice repeated, "Obser-" on sig. T. 1; and "Obser-vations" on Yy. 4ᵇ. The insertion of these important documents, with the Acts of Convocation for 1640, 1661; and for 1586, 1588, was finally made here in order to bring them near to those of 1562, which occupy pp. 191—221.

In primis pro Capite
- A Miter
- A fillet of Lynnen Cloth, ad circum-cingendum cap^{ut} sub Corona(m)[1]
- A Lynnen Cap or Coyfe
- A Round peice of Linnen Cloth like a Trencher to cover his Crowne when it is anoynted
- And a little Quantetie of small Cotten, made Round to lye between his Crowne and the said Round peice of Linnen.

Pro Corpore
- Amict
- Albe
- Stoole[2]
- fanowne
- Dalmatick
- Tunicle
- Chrisible[3]
- A Curtell of White Cloth to the grounde under all these forsaide Vestiments.

Pro manibus
- * A paire of Linnen Gloves   * lf. 17^a.
- A pontificall Ring of cupp^r[4] and gilt with a conterfet stone
- iij Polices[5] of bustian pro Consecratoribus for their thumbes
- A Crosier of tree[6] peynted white.

Pro tibiis
- A pair of Sabatines[7] of bustian with whit Strings to fasten them about his Leggs garterwise.

[1] 'Coronam' *altered to* Corona.

[2] Stoole: *i.e.* a stole.

[3] Chrisible: *i.e.* a chasuble.

[4] cupp^r: *i.e.* copper.

[5] Polices: *i.e.* pollices, or thumb-stalls.

[6] of tree: *i.e.* wooden.

[7] Sabatines, buskins, as in the Coronation of the King.

Pro pedibus {A paire of Sendals of bustian.

Alia necessaria {
A small towell knitt about the Crosier

ij other Larger Towells ad tegendum [1] manus

iij Apornes, for every Busshop one, to kepe clene their Vestiments, in tempore ablucionis capitis et manuum consecrati

Liber pontificalis.

Item preter ista precedentia oportebit consecratum in die consecrationis offerre panem, vinum et ceram, hoc est tortulas cereas.

[As a companion to the extract in § 3, from Lambeth MS. 751, I offer the reader another 16th century list of a somewhat similar character from a fly-leaf at the end of Bp Halam's (15th cent.) register at Salisbury.]

(3*) *Thees be thoo thynges that beeñ necessary for the halowyng of a churche.*

IN primis .ij. laarge fattes full of water.
o0ñ within the churche dore, and
an other with owte.
and iiij laarge treyñ Bolles or Basyns
and a small ladyl of tree.

Item xxiiij wex candelles, euerych of .i. foote longe or more.

Item a dyssh full of salt.
and a dyssh full of aysshes fayre syfte.

Item a quarte of Red Wyne.
and an handfull of ysope.

---

[1] tegendum : *read perhaps* tergendum.

Item small wex Roll Candelles. to make .v. crosses
vpon the awter, yf the awter be to halowyng.
and half a pound of Incense.

Item oon lynnen clothe fayre wasshyn, to make clene
the awters, which cloth after shall be brent,
and a clene treyn cop or dysshe.

Item the church and the chauncell flore most be
clene voyded from dextes and segees, and fayre
swoped with a Besom. I*n* which flore fro the
northe corner of the chauncell to the southe
corner of the churche ende throw all the
churche ; and fro the este corner of the
chauncell dowñ to the west corner of the
churche, ther most be made in the flore or
pament an Andrewes crosse of small sonde
of a foote of Brede, and an ynche thyck atte
leest.

Item .j. Senser with colys.

Item .ij. Elnes of new lynneñ clothe for an Apron
for the Busshoᵽ and for Brachyales.
And also lynneñ clothe suffycyent for Aprons
for his mynysters.

Item .j. short fourme.
with a tapete and Quysshynes to knele at.

And a tent withowt the west ende of the church
yerd made of Clothe in whiche the Busshop
and his mynysters shall be rayed.

All thees thinges above saide. except Sond beeñ
necessary and requysyte aswel in the halowyng
of a churche yerd. by hym selfe. as in the
holowyng of a churche and the awter.
Savyng over this. in the halowyng of a churche-
yerd ther most be ordeyned.

.iiij. laarge crosses of tree of ĩĩj foote of heyghe. whiche most stond fastened in the erthe at iiij corners of the church yerd.

And xij wex tapers to be sot vpoñ euery crosse.

Item at euery corner of the churche yerd. a fatt with fayre water.

———————

Gibson's *Synodus Anglicana*, 8ᵛᵒ· or 12°, 1702, is in Lambeth Library 102. 1. 15.

It contains extracts which Gibson may have derived from MS. 751, or from other earlier registers or originals[1]. To proceed with its contents we find—

(4) The order of sitting in Parliament house and other assemblies provided aº. 31 Hen. VIII. [1539–40][2].

THE Cloth of estate by the side whereof none may sit but the King's children.

Dextra Pars.

The Queen's[3] vicegerent in Ecclesiasticall matters if there be any.

The Lord Archbishop of Canterburie.

The Lord Archbishop of York.

The Bishop of London.

The Bishop of Duresme.

The Bishop of Winchester.

———————

[1] I appear to have examined MS. 751 on 28 Oct. 1896. It is a small 4° of 294 leaves, collected in the 17th—18th century; and it was collated by Gibson and Ro. Thompson.

[2] See *Stat.* 31 Hen. VIII. cap. 10, § 3.   Cited next below.

[3] This copy of the document was Elizabethan, perhaps Abp Parker's.

And so forth all the Bishops of the Province according to their Auncient and old Custom.

If a Bishop be Secretorie, then he shall be placed above all the Bishops having none of the other specified on the left side.

Sinistra Pars.

The Lord Chancellor, &c.   (lf. 19^b—22.)

(The Statute last named runs as follows.)

𝔄𝔫𝔫𝔬 xxxi° 𝔥𝔢𝔫𝔯𝔦𝔠𝔦 VIII. 28 Apr.—28 June, 1539.

Cap. x.   *For placing of the lords.*

4 Inst. 361.] *Forasmuch as in all great councils and congregations of men, having sundry degrees and offices in the commonwealth, it is very requisite and convenient that an order should be had and taken for the placing and sitting of such persons as been bounden to resort to the same....*

II.   First, it is enacted by authority aforesaid, That no person, or persons, of what estate, degree or condition soever he or they be of (except only the King's children) shall at any time hereafter attempt or presume to sit or have place at any side of the cloth of estate in the parliament chamber, neither of the one hand of the King's highness, nor of the other, whether the King's majesty be there personally present or absent.   (2) *And forasmuch as the King's majesty is justly and lawfully supreme head in earth, under God, of the church of* England, *and for the good exercise of the said most royal dignity and office, hath made* Thomas *lord* Crumwel *and lord privy seal, his vicegerent, for good and due ministration of justice to be had in all causes and cases touching the ecclesiastical jurisdiction, and for the godly reformation and redress of all errors, heresies and abuses in the said church;* (3) It is therefore also enacted by authority aforesaid That the said lord *Crumwel*, having the said office of vicegerent, and all other persons which hereafter shall have the said office of the grant of the King's highness, his heirs or successors, shall sit and be placed, as well in this present parliament, as in all parliaments to be holden hereafter, on the right side of the parliament chamber, and upon the same form that the archbishop of *Canterbury* sitteth on, and above the same archbishop and his successors, and shall have voice in every parliament to assent, or dissent, as other the lords of the parliament.

III. And it is also enacted, That next to the said vicegerent shall sit the archbishop of *Canterbury*; and then next to him, on the same form and side, shall sit the archbishop of *York*; and next to him, on the same form and side, the bishop of *London*; and next to him, on the same side and form, the bishop of *Durham*; and next to him, on the same side and form, the bishop of *Winchester*; and then all the other bishops of both provinces of *Canterbury* and *York* shall sit and be placed on the same side after their ancienties, as it hath been accustomed.

[IV. The lord chancellor, president of the King's council and lord privy seal...on the left side of the said parliament chamber, on the highest part of the form of the same side, above all dukes, except only such as shall happen to be the King's son,...brother, ...uncle,...nephew, or the King's brothers' or sisters' sons.]

[V. The great chamberlain, constable, marshal, admiral, grand master or lord steward and chamberlain...shall sit and be placed after the lord privy seal.]

VI. And it is also enacted by authority aforesaid, That the King's chief secretary, being of the degree of a baron of the parliament, shall sit and be placed afore and above all barons, not having any of the offices above mentioned; (2) and if he be a bishop, then he shall sit and be placed above all other bishops not having any of the offices above mentioned.

[VII. All dukes not aforementioned, marquesses, earls, viscounts and barons, not having any of the offices aforesaid, shall sit and be placed after their ancienty, as it hath been accustomed.]

[VIII. The places of great officers under the degree of barons...at the uppermost part of the sacks, in the midst of the said parliament chamber, either there to sit upon one form, or upon the uppermost sack, the one of them above the other, in order as is above rehearsed.]

[IX. Places of the triours in trials by peers.]

[X. Places of the lord chancellor, treasurer, &c. in the Star-chamber, and other assemblies and conferences of council.]

Statutes at Large, Camb. 1763, 8vo. iv. 452–4.

Cf. Phillimore, *Ecclesiastical Law*, ed. 2, 1895, i. 57.

(5) A list of the Bishops aº 1562 and aº 1561. (lf. 22ᵇ, 23.)

(6) A list of Bishoprics, and Offices under the

Bishops in each case, as if intended to be filled up
with the names. (lf. 22ᵇ—35.)

(7) DOMINUS WINTOÑ EPISCOPUS, sede London*iensi* plena, sortitur nomen Subdecani, cujus
nominis pretextu in Congregatione Episcoporum et
cleri sedebit propinquius Archiepiscopo a latere
sinistro, nisi Archiepiscopus Eboracensis fuerit presens, quia tunc idem Archiepiscopus sedebit in parte
dextra Archiepiscopi Cantuarien*sis*, et London*iensis*
Episcopus a parte sinistra. Et do*mi*nus Winton-
iensis proximus London*iensi*. Et sede London*iensi*
vacante, Dominus Winton*iensis* gerit vices Decani
Suffraganeorum Cant*uariensis* provinciæ, (et*interlin.*)
creditur bene quod recipiet mandatum Archiepiscopi
pro clero convocando et pro *commun*ibus processionibus *faciendis.

* f. 36ᵇ.

Sed sede London*iensi* plena, Winton*iensis* de
h*ujus*modi mandatis nihil intromittet, licet London-
iensis absens sive in remotis fuerit.

In Convocatione etiam Cleri, si coram Archiepiscopo cum cetu Ep*iscop*orum missa celebretur ;
si Londin*iensis* missum celebraverit, seu absens
fuerit, Winton*iensis* a celebratore queret pacem, et
Archiep*iscop*o deferet*ur*†.

† *Sic.*

(8) MEMORANDUM quod illo tempore quo Dñus
Rob*er*tus de Winchelse Cant*uariensis* Archiep*iscop*us
fuit per Papam suspensus ab administratione sp*iri*tu-
alium et temporalium Archiep*iscop*atus, Magister
Wil*liel*mus de Testa, nuncius sedis Apostolice in
Anglia, habuit custodiam d*ic*ti Archiep*iscop*atus, et
scripsit dño Henrico Woodlock[1] tunc Winton*iensi*

c. 1306.]

[1] H. de Merewell *alias* Woodlock, prior of St Swithin's Winton
Bp of Winchester, 1306—16.

Episcopo, tanquam Decano Suffraganeorum Can-
tuariensis provincie, sede London*iensi* vacan*te*, ut
ipse Magistrum Stephan*um*[1] de Segrave tunc
D[ecanum][1] London*iensem* electum in ep*iscop*um
consecraret, et sic fecit [25 Nov. 1313, apud
Cantuariam].

(9) ITEM Memorandu*m* quod Henricus Ep*iscop*us
Winton*iensis* coronavit Regem [Edwardum II.,
25 Feb. 1308]. (lf. 35, 36[b].)

(10) Ex *Constitutionibus* Lyndwoode, lib. 5.
De penis, Cap. 1, et erit in glossa.
Habet [namque] Cantuariensis...Cruciferarium.
[*Vide supra*, no. VIII., p. 21.] (lf. 37.)

(11) Feoda solvenda Actuario et Ostiario Infe-
rioris Domus.

(12) Ordo agendi Synodum.
Ex concilio Toletano 3°, cap. 4. (lf. 39.)

(13) Acts of Convocation, 5 Nov. 1529, 1532,
1536, 1541, 1553, 1554-7. (lf. 46[b]—94.)

(14) Do., do. 1558-63. (lf. 187 &c.)

(15) Writs &c. relating to Convocation. (lf.
261.)

(16) A Directorie for the Order to be observed[2]
by my Lord of Canterbury his Grace the first day of
Convocation. [Evidently derived from the Latin
'*Forma sive Descriptio.*'] (lf. 287.)

(17) The Order of Abp Matthew Parker's
Consecration. (lf. 289[b].)

---

[1] *Gilbert* de Segrave, *Precentor* of St Paul's.
[2] Perhaps Abp Parker's Account, mentioned in [Gibson's] *Com-
pleat History of Convocation*, ed. 2, i. p. 23.

(18)   The Manner and Form of Consecrating a Bisshoppe in the Chappell at Lamhithe.   (lf. 293.)

At the end is the note (on lf. 294)

"July 14, 1701.

This Book was collated from beginning to end with yᵉ Original by us

Edmund Gibson
Robert Thompson."

X.   There is an old Table of Precedence preserved at Oxford in MS. Balliol 354, f. C. lxxxxj. = leaf 203, back.   See Dr Furnivall's *Manners and Meals* (Early Engl. Text Soc., 1868), p. 381.

The ordre of goyng
or sittyng

A POPE hath no pere
An emprowre A-lone
A kyng A-lone
An high cardynall
A prince, A kyngis son;
¹[Archebischoppe is to hym per-
   egalle.]
A duke of blod Royall

❡ A busshop
A markes
An erle
❡ A vycownt
²A legate
A baroñ
¹[A Suffrigan]
An abbot mytred
the [i]ij cheff Jugys
the mayor of londoñ

²the chife baroñ of the cheker

[𝕿𝖍𝖊 𝕶𝖓𝖎𝖌𝖍𝖙'𝖘 𝖗𝖆𝖓𝖐:]

❡ ¹[Pryoure Cathedralle]
An Abbot without myter

A knyght [bacheler]
A pryoure
A deañe
An Arche-dekoñ
[A knyght]
[The body Esquyere]
³The Master of the rollis
the vnder Jugis
³[Clerke of the crowne]
the vnder barons of the cheker
the mayor of caleis

A provyncyall
A doctour of diuinite

¹ Inserted from Russell's *Book of Nurture*, ed. Furnivall, 186.
² Omitted in W. de Worde's *Boke of Keruynge*, ibid. 288.
³ These additions are taken from a very similar order ('*The Office*

A prothonotary ys boue [1]
the popes colectour

[**Squire's rank :**]
⁋ A doctur of both lawes

[2][Ex-mayor, a Londoner]
A sergeant[3] of lawe

the Masters of Chaunsery
[2][Pardoners coming to preach]
[2][Clerkes that hañ taken degre]
[2][ordurs of religion]

A persoñ of Chyrch
A seculer prest
A marchañt

oj a connynge Vschere or Marshalle'), in verse, contained in the *Boke of Nurture* of J. Russell, gentleman usher to Duke Humphrey about 1440. See Furnivall's *Manners and Meals*, pp. 185—7; cf. pp. 188—9, their Order of Dining in Chamber Hall, &c. The precedence of graduates of the university, and other Clergy, and some others, is treated in Russell's book. *Ibid.* pp. 187, 284—5. "An archebysshop and a duke may not kepe the hall, but eche estate by them selfe in chaumbre or in pauylyon, that nether se other."

"Bysshoppes, Marques, Erles, and Vycountes, all these may sit two at a messe." *The Boke of Keruynge*, printed by Wynken de Worde in 1508 and 1513. (*Ibid.* 284—6.)
"Yeff the bischoppe of the provynce of Caunturbury
Be in the presence of the archebischoppe of Yorke reuerently
Their seruice shalle be kouered, eche bisshoppe syngulerly
And in the presence of the metropolytane none other sicurly.
Yeff bischopps of Yorke provynce be fortune be syttynge
In the presence of the primate of Englond thañ beynge,
They must be couered in all theyr seruynge,
And not in the presence of the bischoppe of Yorke there apperynge."
Russell's *Boke of Nurture* in 'Manners and Meals,' p. 189.
After masters of chancery, rank as follows :—
"The worshipfulle prechoure of pardoun in that place to appere.
The clerkes of connynge that hañ takeñ degre,
And all othur ordurs of chastite chosyñ, and also of pouerte,
All parsons and vicaries that ar of dignyte,
Parische prestes kepynge cure, vn-to them loke ye se.
For the baliffes of a Cite purvey ye must a space,
A yemañ of the crowne, Sargeaunt of armes with mace,
A herrowd of Armes as gret as a dygnyte has
Specially kynge harrawd, must haue the principalle place,
Worshipfulle merchaundes and riche artyficeris,
Gentilmeñ welle nurtured and of good maneris,
With gentilwommen, and namely lordes nurrieris."
(Cf. p. 226) *Ibid.* p. 187.

[1] boue : *i.e.* 'above.'   [2] See note 3 on pp. 32, 33.
[3] 'seruaunt,' p. 284 : presumably for *'serieaunt.'*

A gentylmañ [All these may   An Artificer
sit at the squyers table]   A yeman of gode name

XI. ENTHRONISATION of J. MORTON, Abp of
Canterbury, Jan. (? 28), 1486–7.

THE Archbishop and all other Prelates went into
the Vestry.

The Bp of Ely was Deken and rede the Gospel.

The Bishop of Roch[ester] bar the Crosse and
redde thespistel, and

The Bp of Saresbury was Channter and begunne
the office of the Masse.

J. Leland, *Collectanea*, ed. T. Hearne, 1770, iv. 208.

XII. BURIAL SERVICE for PRINCE ARTHUR, 1502.

THE second Masse of the Trinitie was songe by
the bishoppe of Salisbury and the queere, without
orgaines or children ; and at the Masse the Earle of
Surrey offred a piece of gould and v. *s.* for the Masse
pennye.

Leland, *Collectanea*, v. 376.   D. Rock,
Church of our Fathers, edd. Hart and
Frere, ii. 405 (= 504) *n.*

[We come next to Abp Parker's statement as to
the precedence and relative duties of the Bishops of
London and Winchester.]

XIII. M. PARKER, '*De Antiquitate*,' 1572.

PRIMVS itaque sub Primate honos Londinensi
episcopo delatus est. Is, in Synodo et Collegio
Episcoporum Cantuariensi, provinciæ Decanus dictus
est. Qui quicquid a Metropolitano decretum per
provinciam suam mandabatur, litteris suis ad in-
feriores præsules exequutus, debitæ suæ exequutionis

eundem per litteras mandato remisso fecit certiorem.
Itaque, per hunc, et tocius provinciæ clerus ad
Synodos celebrandas conuocari, et legitima primatis
sui monitu peragere consuevit. Tum in profligatis
illis papisticis ritibus pomposis atque solemnibus, in
Synodis et conuentibus cleri, coram Archiepiscopo
fuit Missidicus. Ob quæ summa munera, in Synodis
et sessionibus Episcoporum, proximus illi Archiepiscopo locus a dexteris concessus est, nisi Eboracensis adesset, quo interveniente, et a dextris sedente,
Londiniensis sinistras obtinuit.

W. Lind-
wood.
Lib. 5 *de*
pœnis,
Cap.
Æternæ
sanctio.
Et ex
Archivis.

Post Londiniensem Wintoniensis in summo
honore apud Primatem fuit, quia Cancellarius ejus
nominabatur. Hujus munus fuit, in missis in
Synodo per Londiniensem celebratis auream pacem
accipere, eandemque ad Archiepiscopum osculandam
deferre, et altari referre.

Sed et Londoniensi sede vacante, Episcopove in
remotis agente, Wintoniensis ejus vices suscepit,
et Subdecanus Cantuariensis provinciæ dicebatur.
Hujusque honoris causa, ut Londoniensis dextras,
sic Wintoniensis sinistras Archiepiscopi proximus
occupavit.

Sed Eboracensi præsente a sinistris propter
Londoniensem sedebat. Quam grata autem fuissent
suffraganeis hæc honoris officia, sub primate suo
gesta, ex Johannis Pountois Winton Episcopi literis
Richardi Gravesend tunc Episcopi Londoniensis
mortui vices agentis, ad †Johannem Peckham† Cantuariensem Archiepiscopum scriptis apparet.

Epistola Johannis Winton: ad †Johannem
Peckham† Cantuariensem Archiepiscopum.

†—† Surely Jo. Peckham is a mistake for Robertum Winchelsey,
as the date is about Dec. 1303.

Ex archē-
tycho (sic).
Anno
1284. [Ed.
1605,
p. 21.]

Ex Florilegi] Reverendissimo &c....Capellanus vester Wintoniensis [*ut supra*, no. VI.].

Nam præter dictas eminentias et prærogativas, etiam reges a Londoniensibus et Wintoniensibus Episcopis, Archiepiscopis Cantuariensibus mortuis vel absentibus, tanquam eorum vicariis in coronatione vngi et sacrari solebant. Qua ratione Edwardus rex, ejus nominis II. ab Henrico Woodlock Wintoniensi Episcopo consecratus fuit, absentis Archiepiscopi mandato, quod Robertus Winchelsey tunc Archiepiscopus ab exilio, in quod ab Edwardo I. actus est, nondum reversus fuerat, vt in vita ejusdem Roberti deinceps declarabitur.

Post Wintoniensem, Lincolniensis Vicecancellarius fuit:

Tum Salisburiensis Praecentor: deinde, Wigorniensis Capellanus: et

Roffensis Cruciger Metropolitani, fuerunt. Quibus honoribus et primati suo arctius deuinciebantur, et præ cæteris illustriores habebantur.

Atque hoc in loco commodum est, eas quoque præfecturas, quas in sessionibus supremi concilii, quod Parliamentum dicitur, vtriusque provinciæ tenent Episcopi, recensere.

Primo itaque loco sedet Cantuariensis:

2°. Eboracensis Archiepiscopus;

3°. Londoniensis Episcopus,

4°. Dunelmensis,

5°. Wintoniensis, qui et nobilitati illius ordinis in Anglia Garterii Prælatus procerum illius ordinis, interiori semper adest consilio.

Reliqui post hos 5 Episcopos sine sedum suarum discrimine, vt consecracione priores, ita locis potiores et digniores censentur.

Quod si quis Episcoporum regi fuerit a secretis, is post 5 Episcopos prædictos primus locum capit.

Matt. Parker, *De Antiquitate Britannicæ Ecclesiæ, et Privilegiis Ecclesiæ Cantuariensis*, fo. 1574, pp. 24—5[1].

[In Abp Parker's book—the first which was privately printed in England—he was assisted by his Secretaries G. Ackworth and J. Josseline. The copy presented to Q. Elizabeth is now in the British Museum. Its woodcut borders were illuminated, and it was sumptuously bound in embroidered velvet, and contains some of its pages printed on vellum.]

When the number of English bishoprics was increased by the final constitution of the see of Manchester (10 Aug. 1847), it was enacted with reference to the seats for Bishops in the House of Lords, that

THE number of lords spiritual now sitting and voting as lords of parliament shall not be increased by the creation of the bishoprick of *Manchester*[2]; and whenever there shall be a vacancy among the lords spiritual by the avoidance of any one of the sees of *Canterbury, York, London, Durham*, or *Winchester*, or of any other see which shall be filled by the translation thereto from any other see of a bishop at that time actually sitting as a lord of parliament, such vacancy shall be supplied by the issue of a writ of summons to the bishop who shall be elected to the same see; but if such vacancy be caused by avoidance of any other see in

---

[1] In the edition of 1605, the foregoing passage occurs on pp. 20, 21.

[2] "by the creation of a new bishoprick." *Bishoprics Act*, 1878, 41 & 42 Vict. c. lxviii. s. 5.

England or *Wales*, such vacancy shall be supplied by the issue of a writ of summons to that bishop of a see[1] in *England* or *Wales* who shall not have previously[2] become entitled to such writ ; and no bishop who shall be hereafter elected to any see in *England* or *Wales*, not being one of the five sees above named, shall be entitled to have a writ of summons, unless in the order and according to the conditions above prescribed.

Stat. 10 & 11 Vict. c. cviii. s. 2.

Similar provisions are contained in the Acts for St Albans and Truro, 38 & 39 Vict. c. xxxiv.; and 38 & 39 Vict. c. liv.

The Bishoprics Act, 1878, 41 & 42 Vict. c. 68, has the further *proviso* :—" Provided that where a bishop is translated from one see to another, and was at the date of his translation actually sitting as a lord of parliament, he shall not thereupon lose his right to receive a writ of summons to parliament."

[In the account of St Osmund of Salisbury given by J. W[ilson, otherwise Watson] in " *The English Martyrologe*, conteyning a svmmary of the lives of the glorious and renowned Saintes of the three Kingdomes...By a Catholicke Priest," 8vo. 1608, the following interesting statement is preserved.]

XIV.   The English Martyrologe, 1608.

At *Salisbury* in *Wiltshire* the Translation of S. Osmund, Confessor and Bishop of the same Seat†,

---

[1-2] "in *England* who having been longest bishop of a see in *England* has not previously":—*Bishoprics Act*, 1878. See Phillimore's *Eccl. Law*, i. 56. A bishop confirmed may sit in parliament as a lord thereof. (*Ibid.*) Gibson, 128.   † *Sic.*

whose life and doctrine hath much illustrated as well the universall as our Catholicke Church of England.

He was the first that compiled the *Sarū Breviary* and other Cerimonies of that Church, which were afterward receuyed and vsed throughout the whole Realme.

For which cause in ancient tymes the Catholicke Bishops of *Salisbury* obtayned the Titles of the *Popes* Maister of the Cerimonyes, and had their places alwayes assigned them in the Popes Chappell and other soleñityes at *Rome*, according to that dignity.

> *The English Martyrologe*, 1608 (at July 16th), p. 194. (The last paragraph is omitted in the 3rd edition, published in 1667.)

XV. Forma sive Descriptio Convocationis Celebrandæ, prout ab antiquo celebrari consuevit. 4°. Londini, 1702.

See above, no. IX., pp. 22, 30.

XVI. JOHN JOHNSON, 'Clergy-Man's *Vade-Mecum*,' 1705, &c.

SOME are very positive that the Elections [of Proctors for the Convocation] ought to be made by Virtue of the *Præmunientes* Clause, and that every Bishop should give his *Mandate* to the Archdeacons and Deans, to proceed in their Elections, by Authority thereof; but the generality have and do proceed in obedience to a *Mandate*, sent from

the Archbishop to the Bishop of *London*, Dean of
the Province, and by him to the rest of the Bishops,
and by them to their Deans and Chapters, and Archdeacons, to chuse Proctors to appear at St *Paul*'s in
Convocation.

> *The Clergy-Man's* Vade-Mecum, i. 146—7,
> ed. 3, 1709, 12mo = p. 40, ed. 4, 1715.

XVII. [Edmund Gibson, Bp of Lincoln, 1716–20;
 Bp of London, 1720–48.] ON THE METHOD
 OF SUMMONING AN ENGLISH CONVOCATION.

THE Archbishop is only *Licens'd* or *Directed* to
Exert a Power and Authority which belongs to him,
as well in the common Right of a Metropolitan, as
by the antient Laws and Customs of this Realm.
In virtue whereof, he directs his *Mandate* to the
Bishop of *London*, whose Office it is, as his Grace's
Dean of the Province, to *Execute* that *Mandate*,
and whose part therefore in the calling a *Convocation*,
answers to that of the Lord Chancellor, in the
Summons of a Parliament. Both of them [viz. Lord
Chancellor, and Bishop of London the Dean of the
Province] act *Ministerially* in the *Name* and by the
Authority, the one of his *Civil*, and the other of his
Ecclesiastical Superior.

> *A Compleat History of Convocations*, from
> 1356 to 1689. [By Bp Gibson] ed. 2,
> 1730, pp. 17—18.

XVIII. T. LATHBURY, *History of Convocation*, 1842, &c.

THE writ of Convocation is ordered by the Lord Chancellor, prepared by the Clerk of the Crown, and then transmitted to the Archbishop, who issues his mandate to the Bishop of London as Dean of the province of Canterbury.

During a vacancy of the see of London, the mandate is sent to the Bishop of Winchester as Subdean.

History of Convocation, ed. 2, p. 118, 8vo. 1853.

[When I held a curacy at Alvechurch in the diocese of Worcester in 1875, I came across a statement in some local history or guide-book, in part supported by the *Worcester Diocesan Church Calendar* for 1875[1], p. 66, to the effect that the arms of the see of Worcester (Argent : ten torteaux, four, three, two, and one)[2] represented either coins—but these, I suppose, would have been indicated by bezants—or else hosts upon a paten, and indicated that the bishop of that diocese was Treasurer, or else Sacrist, of the Provincial Chapter of Canterbury, and that the number 10 was connected with the number of suffragan sees in the province in days of old. Being somewhat sceptical about the statement, I sought the more trustworthy opinion of Dr Benson, at that time Chancellor of Lincoln. I give so much of his reply as concerns this question :—]

---

[1] The editors of the Worcester Calendar for 1875 were the Rev. R. Lawson, Rector of Upton-on-Severn, J. Howe, Vicar of Knowle, and J. C. Blissard, Incumbent of St Augustine's, Edgbaston.

[2] "torteaux;...or rather 'hosts,' in allusion to the Bishop [of Worcester]'s privilege of celebrating mass before the College of Bishops," *l.c.* 66 *n.*

XIX.   Dr E. W. Benson to the Rev. Chr. Wordsworth, M.A., Assistant Curate at Alvechurch.

The Chancery [Lincoln].
7 June, 1875.

My dear Wordsworth,

Thank you for the compline card very much [published by Messrs Longhurst]. I quite agree with you that the alterations are not improvements in point of devotional taste. But the idea seems a good one....I was occupied in reading your book. The Master of Trinity told me he had found one mistake....

About the arms of Worcester, I can't believe that it has anything to do with 10 Hostiæ. There were never only 10 Bishops of this Province, except, I think, in the 7th or 8th century—and I am not sure of that. Certainly, never after Heraldry began. These must, I think, be really the arms of Bp Giffard [1268–1303] adopted for the see, as Bp Cantelupe's were for Hereford. I have read and much liked Vernon Hutton's pamphlet. Very good sense, I think [*&c., &c.*].

Ever yours affectionately,

E. W. BENSON.

XX.   The Lincoln Diocesan Church Calendar ...for the years 1874–79.

The Bishop of Lincoln bears the honorary title of Chancellor of the Province of Canterbury. The origin of this distinction is obscure and its meaning not very certain ; Archbishop Parker gives him the title of Vice-Chancellor, and places him third in order among the provincial dignitaries : the Bishops of London and Winchester preceding, and those of Salisbury, Worcester, and Rochester following.

Lincoln Diocesan Calendar, ii. p. iv.

[In the 'Lincoln Diocesan Calendar for 1880,' published in the 11th year of my Father's episcopate, with his sanction the foregoing paragraph was discarded in favour of the following :—]

XXI. LINCOLN DIOCESAN CALENDAR for 1880–84.

ACCORDING to Archbishop Parker (*Antiq. Britann.* pp. 20, 21) the Bishop of Lincoln bears the honorary title of Vice-Chancellor of the Province of Canterbury. The Bishops of the Province were regarded as forming a College, of which the Bishop of London was Dean, and the Bishops of Winchester, Lincoln, Salisbury, Worcester, and Rochester had respectively the titles of Chancellor, Vice-Chancellor, Precentor, Chaplain, and Crucifer, the Bishop of Lincoln holding the third place among the Suffragans of Canterbury.

[In the *Lincoln Diocesan Calendar* for 1885 and subsequent years the paragraph on this subject has been omitted altogether.]

[In Debrett's *Illustrated Peerage*, 1883, only one prelate sets forth his claim to an official position in the Provincial College, viz.:—]

XXII. Debrett's Peerage, 1883.

Salisbury, Lord Bishop of. (Moberly)...conse-
crated 92nd Bishop of Salisbury, 1869; is Provincial
Precentor of Canterbury.

Illustrated Peerage, p. 590.

[In Crockford's *Clerical Directory* during the last
thirty years more claims have been put forward.]

XXIII. Crockford's 'Clerical Directory,'
1874–1904.

1874. *London.* Right Reverend John Jackson,
Lord Bishop of London...is Provincial
Dean of Canterbury. (So also for 1877,
and, *mutatis mutandis*, for 1893 and 1899;
and on p. lxxvii. for 1904.)

,, *Oxford.* Right Reverend John Fielder
Mackarness, Lord Bishop of Oxford...is
Chancellor of the Most Noble Order of
the Garter. (So also for 1877, 1893, 1899,
1904.)

,, *Salisbury.* Right Reverend George Moberly,
Lord Bishop of Sarum...is Provincial Pre-
centor of the Province of Canterbury.
(So also for 1877, 1893, 1899, 1904.)

, *Winchester.* Right Reverend Edward Harold
Browne, Lord Bishop of Winchester...is
Prelate of the Most Noble Order of the
Garter; Provincial Chancellor of Canterbury. (So also for 1877; and similarly for
1893, 1899, 1904, inserting the words "*ex
officio*" (Prelate)....)

1890. *Lincoln*. Right Reverend Edward King, Lord Bishop of Lincoln...is also Provincial Chancellor of Canterbury. (So for 1893, 1899, 1904.)

,, *Rochester*. Right Reverend Anthony Wilson Thorold [Lord Bishop of Rochester]...is Provincial Chaplain of Canterbury[1]. (So also, *mutatis mutandis*, for 1893, 1899, 1904.)

,, *Worcester*. Right Reverend Henry Philpott, Lord Bishop of Worcester...Provincial Chaplain of Canterbury. (So also for 1893, 1899, and on p. lxxxix. for 1904.)

[The Bishop of Bristol notes that some confusion has arisen as to the position and office held by certain Prelates in the Provincial College.]

XXIV. THE BISHOP OF BRISTOL TO THE BISHOP OF LINCOLN, 1905.

13th Oct. 1905.

MY DEAR BROTHER AND FATHER,

...I am told that *Lincoln* has been regarded as Chancellor and Chaplain....In one list, which I have, Worcester is Chancellor; and Winchester, Chaplain (*&c.*, *&c.*).

G. F. BRISTOL.

[As to the last sentence, it seems most probable that the names 'Winchester' and 'Worcester' had

---

[1] The Bp of Rochester is styled "Provincial Chaplain *to the Archbishop of Canterbury*" in Crockford's *Directory*, 1890, p. lviii.; 1893, p. lviii.; and 1899, p. lviii. And, in 1904, p. lxxxvi., "*Cross-earer to the Archbishop of Canterbury.*"

been indistinctly written, or misread, in the copy
from which the list mentioned by the Bishop of
Bristol has been transcribed. I never heard, while
I was at Lincoln, that the Bishop of Lincoln had
been supposed to be a Chaplain in the Provincial
College. My Father was of opinion that he was
Chancellor, relying no doubt on no. vi., p. 17 above,
and so Abp Benson had thought, but he was led to
modify that opinion in 1886.]

It is true no doubt that a Bp of Winchester
(J. de Pontissara) in 1303 signed himself "your
Grace's *Chaplain*" (no. v.).   But this, I take it,
any suffragan of Canterbury might have done,
especially if he were personally intimate with the
Primate or had at one time actually stood in such a
relation to the Abp, much as Dr Benson (afterwards
Primate), in familiar letters to my Father, used to
subscribe himself (1876), "Your most affectionate
faithful Bedesman, My dear Lord,—E. W. Benson."

[The Order for the Proceeding at the Coronation
of Their Majesties K. Edward VII. and Q. Alexandra
was issued by the Earl Marshal about 5th June,
1902, with a view to the Service announced for
June 26th. In consequence of His Majesty's serious
illness, the Coronation was postponed until Saturday,
the Eve of St Lawrence, 9th Aug. 1902.

As records of this kind are apt to be mislaid,
I include in the present paper the names of the
Bishops, who, upon one ground or another, were
distinguished on that occasion by a place of special
dignity in the order of Procession.]

XXV. The PROCEEDING for the CORONATION
at Westminster, 1902.

From the West Door of the Abbey into the Choir.

Chaplains in Ordinary.
Sub-Dean of the Chapels Royal.
Rev. Canon F. A. J. Hervey.   Very Rev. Dean of Windsor.
The Prebendaries of Westminster.
Dean of Westminster.
Pursuivants.
Officers of the Orders of Knighthood.
Prelate of the Order of
St Michael and St George (Abp of *Rupertsland*).
&c. &c. &c.
The Lord Chancellor of Ireland,
attended by his Purse-bearer; his Coronet carried by his Page.
The Lord Archbishop of *York*,
attended by a gentleman (Eric Maclagan, Esq.).
The Lord High Chancellor,
attended by his Purse-bearer; his Coronet carried by his Page.
The Lord Archbishop of *Canterbury*,
attended by two gentlemen (F. C. and W. Temple, Esqs.).
Portcullis Pursuivant.   Windsor Herald.   Rouge Dragon Pursuivant.

THE QUEEN'S REGALIA
The Ld Chamberlain
of Her M. Household

The Ivory Rod with the Dove &c. &c.	&c. Her Majesty's Crown borne, &c.	The Sceptre with the Cross &c. &c.
The Bishop of *Oxford* &c. &c.	THE QUEEN Her Majesty's train &c. &c.	The Bishop of *Norwich* &c. &c.

(left margin: Sub-Officer and Five Gentlemen-at-Arms. *)*
(right margin: Clerk of the Cheque and Adjutant and Five Gentlemen-at-Arms. *)*

THE KING'S REGALIA
St Edward's Staff   The Sceptre with the Cross
&c. &c.   &c. &c.
The Earl Marshal   The Lord High Constable
attended   attended
The Sceptre with   St Edward's   The Orb
the Dove &c.   Crown   &c.
borne by the Lord
High Steward
attended

The Patina, borne by the Bishop of *Ely*	The Bible, borne by the Bishop of *London* [appointed Preacher][1]	The Chalice, borne by the Bishop of *Winchester*
The Bishop of *Bath and Wells*	THE KING in his Royal Crimson Robe of State (&c.) His Majesty's train borne (&c.) &c. &c. &c. &c.	The Bishop of *Durham*

Standard Bearer and Ten Gentlemen-at-Arms, with &c.

Lieutenant and Ten Gentlemen-at-Arms, with &c.

Exons.   Clerk of the Cheque.   Exons.
Twenty Yeomen of the Guard.

[Here it may be noted that the Archbishop of *York* was appointed (probably on account of the great age of the Primate of all England) to crown Her Majesty the Queen. There was, so far as I am aware, no precedent for an Archbishop of York being so honoured[2].

The Archbishop of *Canterbury* crowned His Majesty the King according to the most antient precedents.]

Abp Sancroft's note, made for the Coronation of K. James II. and his Consort in 1685, is clear, in his autograph copy (St John's Coll. Cam., MS. L. 14):—

¶ The Person that is to anoint, & crown yᵉ Kg̃ (& so yᵉ Qu. also) is yᵉ Ld Ap of Cant. *K. Ja.*

¶ The Ap is also to nominate, & appoint the Bp̄s, who are to perform yᵉ following Services at yᵉ Coronation.

1.   Two Bishops to support yᵉ Queen[3].

---

[1] The Sermon was omitted at the postponed Coronation in 1902.

[2] See a paper by Mr L. Wickham Legg, *On the Right of the Abp f York*, &c.   *S. Paul's Eccl. Soc. Trans.* v. 77—84.

[3] Presumably K. James II. had desired the Abp to undertake the

2. Two B̃p̃s to support yᵉ Kg̃, if yᵉ B̃p̃s of Durham & Bath & Wells be õ¹ there. *L.*

3. A Bishop to preach yᵉ Sermon.

[4.] A B̃p̃ to read yᵉ petition of yᵉ B̃p̃s.

[5.] Two B̃p̃s to sing yᵉ Litanie².

[6.] If there be a Cõmunion
{
A B̃p̃ to read yᵉ Epistle

A B̃p̃ to read yᵉ Gospell³

A B̃p̃ to carry yᵉ Regal; (i. S. Edwd̃s stone chalice) &

A B̃p̃ to carry the patin: sc. in yᵉ procession

Four B̃p̃s to hold yᵉ Towell, Two before yᵉ Kg̃ at the Cõmunion: & Two before yᵉ Qu.
}

¶ The Æ̃P is also (∧ 'or yᵉ D[ean] of Westm̃r, if he be a B̃p̃' *interlin.*) to hallow ('consecratt' *interlin.*) yᵉ Oil wherewith yᵉ Kg̃. & Qu. are to be Anointed, setting it upon yᵉ Altar at Westm̃r.

But yᵉ Oil is to be prepar'd by yᵉ Kg̃s physitians.

(St John's Coll. Cam., MS. L. 14.)

I edited, in 1892, for the Henry Bradshaw Society (*Coron. of K. Charles I.*, p. 4), "Sir Theodore Mayhern's Receit" for the coronation oil of 1626. It was "a very fragrant cream," hallowed by Bp Laud, acting for the Bp who was Dean of Westminster; but when, in Dec. 1901, Mr Leopold

selection. The King's own supporters are fixed by long-standing claim.   '¹ õ=non.

² "Two Bishops, or two of the Quire to be appointed to sing yᵉ Litany in yᵉ Quire." *Coronation of K. Charles I.*, p. 4 (from his own copy, St John's Coll. Camb. MS. L. 15), cf. p. 27 *n.*

³ "The Bishop that reads the Gospell must provide Bread and Wine for yᵉ King to offer at yᵉ Communion." *Ibid.*

Wickham Legg had the recipe made up by Mr
Squire, the King's Druggist, and exhibited it to
the St Paul's Ecclesiological Society in the Chapter-
House, it was found to be too sweet and sickly for
twentieth-century nostrils.   Antony Wood has re-
corded that K. Charles II. (like Q. Mary Tudor)
procured "oyl or ointment sent from France, where
it was by a Popish Bishop consecrated." (*Life and
Times*, i. 399.)   For K. James II., his physician
and apothecary, James St Amand, prepared a
fragrant cream, which was "solemnly consecrated
in the morning by the Dean [Bp Sprat of Rochester],
assisted by the Prebendaries[1]."   James II. received
absolution from Rome for receiving unction from an
Anglican prelate[2].   At some coronations (so the late
Mr W. Maskell thought) simple olive oil was used.
But in 1902 (I am credibly informed) it was a com-
pound oil.   It has always happened since 1540 that
the Dean, or at least one of the Prebendaries or
Canons of Westminster, has been a Bishop, though
at Queen Victoria's Coronation Bp Monk, a prebendary, was taken ill, and two other Bishops in that
Chapter had died just before.   It is their duty to see
that the oil is hallowed in the morning of the Coronation Day (by the Archbishop, if they have not a
Bishop *de gremio capituli*).   In 1902 it was done by
a Bishop in the Chapter.

  1.   The King, by antient custom, appoints two
Bishops to support his Royal Consort[3].   *Missale
Westm.* ii. 709, 726.

---

[1] Fra. Sandford, *Hist. of the Coron. of James II.*, 1687, p. 91 *n.*
[2] *Coronation of K. Charles I.*, p. xxxix.
[3] The Queen's supporters in 1761 were J. Thomas, Bp of Lincoln,

2. The Bishop of Durham and the Bishop of Bath and Wells claim the honour of supporting the King on his right hand and on his left, as of very antient right, dating from the time of K. Richard I. (Cf. *Missale Westmonast.* ii. 678–9, iii. 1519; *Chronicon Rogeri Hovedene*, ed. Stubbs, iii. 9.) Their petition should be jointly made. For when, in 1689, Bp Ken put in his claim singly, and Nat. Lord Crewe, the Bishop of Durham (who had been specially subservient to K. James), did not join in the application, the Court of Claims, acting for William and Mary, took occasion to decline to consider the separate petition; and Peter Mew, Bishop of Winchester, and Jonathan Trelawney, Bishop of Bristol, supported "the King and Queen" on the Coronation Day[1].

In later times the claim of the two Bishops (Durham and Bath and Wells) has been re-affirmed and allowed. In 1727, when the Bishopric of Bath and Wells was vacant by the death of Dr G. Hooper, George II., on the petition of the Bp W. Talbot of Durham, assented to the claim of Durham, and consented that the Bp of St Asaph (Dr J. Wynne, who was designated for the vacancy at Wells a few months later) should on that occasion be associated with him in the service of supporters.

3. A Bishop to preach the short Sermon ('*breviter*') to the People at the Coronation is

and T. Hayter, Bp of Norwich. In 1902, the Bishops of Norwich and Oxford. (In 1685, K. James II. left the selection to Abp Sancroft.)

[1] *Collections Relative to Claims at the Coronations,* 8vo. 1820, pp. 54—5. The Heralds' MS., L. 19, supposes that the Bishops of 'Duresm(e)' and Bath and Wells were the supporters as usual. J. W. Legg, *Three Coronation Orders,* 18, 19.

appointed of antient custom by the Archbishop
Metropolitan. *Missale Westm.* ii. 684. In 1626,
Senhouse, Bp of Carlisle, preached on *Rev.* ii. 10. In
1902 the Bishop of London was appointed; but, in
consequence of King Edward's recent illness, the
Sermon was, on that occasion, omitted.

In 1377, T. de Brintone, Bp of Rochester, was the
preacher.

1485, John Russell, Bp of Lincoln.

1547, T. Cranmer, Abp of Canterbury.

1553, J. Scory, Bp of Chichester.

1603, T. Bilson, Bp of Winchester.

1626, Ri. Senhouse, Bp of Carlisle.

1661, G. Morley, Bp of Worcester.

1685, Fra. Turner, Bp of Ely.

1689, Gilbert Burnet, Bp of Salisbury.

1702, John Sharp, Abp of York.

1714, W. Talbot, Bp of Oxford.

1727, John Potter, Bp of Oxford.

1761, Ro. Hay Drummond, Bp of Salisbury.

1821, Hon. E. V. V. Harcourt, Abp of York.

1831, C. J. Blomfield, Bp of London[1].

1838, C. J. Blomfield, Bp of London.

1902 [A. F. Winnington-Ingram, Bp of London,
excused.]

4. A Bishop to read the Petition. The question
"*Si leges et consuetudines,* &c." leading up to the
King's Oath, may be read by the Metropolitan, or
by one of the Bishops (*ibid.* ii. 684). It is usually

---

[1] Dean Stanley's note (*Hist. Memor. Westm.* ed. 1868, p. 49) that
"the Bishop of London has usually preached," though somewhat
inaccurate, may probably be taken as evidence that he recollected
this happening *twice*. And in ed. 1876 Dr Stanley omitted the statement.

done by the Archbishop. (See *Coron. of K. Charles I.*,
pp. 18 foll.) But the '*Requisitio sive Admonitio
Episcoporum ad Regem.* Domine Rex, a vobis per-
donari,' &c., to which Sancroft's note plainly refers,
is assigned to "One of ye Bishops" (*ibid.* p. 23 ;
Missale Westm. ii. 685). In 1485 it was recited by
J. Russell, Bp of Lincoln ; in 1626 by Dr J. Bucke-
ridge, Bishop of Rochester. Since 1689 the under-
taking to maintain the Rights and Privileges of the
Bishops, Clergy, and Church of England has been
included in the Coronation Oath, administered by
the Archbishop. (The 1702 *Declaration*—made
from 1821 onwards, in the presence of the two
Houses of Parliament—is not now made in the
Abbey, but is signed at an earlier date after the
Accession.)

5. Two Bishops to sing the Litany. '*Duo
episcopi vel duo cantores.*' So Laud in 1626. *Missale
Westm.* ii. 687. In 1902, in consequence of the
King's recent illness, the Litany was, I believe, said
at an earlier hour, in Chapter. In 1626, T. Morton,
Bp of Lichfield, and Lewis Baylye, Bp of Bangor,
were chosen. In 1761, the Litany was sung by
Dr Edmund Keene, Bp of Chester (who also, by
the way, was the Gospeller, or bearer of the Chalice),
and Sir W. Ashburnham, Bp of Chichester.

The Archbishop himself rose up to say the
special clauses in the Litany. (*Missale Westm.*
iii. 1520.)

6. A Bishop to read the Epistle. In 1626,
Dr Theophilus Field, Bp of Llandaff, was Epistoler ;
in 1902, Lord Alwyne Compton, Bp of Ely. The
Epistoler brings the Bread upon the Paten from

St Edward's Chapel to the King, for His Majesty to offer by the hands of the Archbishop. The Epistoler is one of those who receive the Holy Communion at the Coronation.

7. A Bishop to read the Gospel. In 1626, the Gospeller was Dr Samuel Harsnett, Bp of Norwich. In 1902, Dr Randall Davidson, at that time Bp of Winchester. The Gospeller brings the Wine in the Chalice from St Edward's Chapel and delivers it to the King, for His Majesty to offer by the hands of the Archbishop, who reverently places it upon the Altar. (*Missale Westm.* ii. 716.) In mediæval times the chalice and paten used for the King's oblation were those of St Edward, the *calix lapideus cum sua patena*, and were not the same as those used at the sacring of the mass, which were of gold. *Missale Westm.* ii. 716 *n.*

8. "A Bishop to carry the Regal (that is, Edward's stone Chalice) in the procession."

† *sic.*   9. "A Bishop to carry the Patin †; *scilicet* in the procession."—Laud, apparently, distinguishes these offices from those of the Gospeller and Epistoler[1], by whom, I believe, they have been performed at modern coronations. In the Proceeding, immediately in front of the King's Canopy, in 1761, the Chalice was borne by Dr Edmund Keene, Lord Bishop of Chester, at whose left side walked Dr Zachary Pearce, Lord Bishop of Rochester (and Dean of Westminster), bearing the

---

[1] In 1626, "The Bp of London (G. Monteigne) carried yᵉ golden (*sic*) Cup for yᵉ Communion; and yᵉ Bp of Winchester (L. Andrewes) yᵉ golden plate" in the procession, Theophilus Field and S. Harsnet, Llandaff and Norwich, being, on that occasion, Epistoler and Gospeller. *Coron. of K. Charles I.*, pp. 85, 87.

Paten. In 1902, in like manner, the Bishop of Winchester bore the Chalice, and the Bp of Ely the Paten; but between them walked the Bishop of London (who would have been the Preacher if there had been a sermon) bearing the Bible.

10. Two Bishops to hold the silken Towel before the King, and two Bishops to hold it before the Queen, at the time of Communion. Laud mentions that in 1626 the "towell of white silke" was duly brought, but that the "faire Ordinarye Towell wch he vses att White Hall was brought to[o], and held before hime bye..." (*names not inserted*). St John's Coll. Cam. MS. L. 12. The Queen was not crowned, nor did she communicate in 1626, though the service was originally drafted to allow for this. This ceremony of the Cloth or Towel was not dropped until 1831. Maskell, *Mon. Rit.* ii. 144 *n.*

11. In antient times the pax, for the kiss of peace, was brought to the King and Queen by him *qui librum evangelii ante detulerat* (*Missale Westm.* ii. 720).

12. On the eighth day after the Coronation a Bishop used to say a mass of the Holy Trinity before the King in the [Abbey] Church, or in the Chapel Royal, and afterwards to remove the linen coif from His Majesty's anointed head. (*ibid.* ii. 698.)

13. At the benediction of Royal Ornaments, at the Coronation, Bishops used to present His Sword to the King. (*ibid.* ii. 699.) This was done in 1902.

In former times the Stone Chalice of St Edward used to be carried, of right, by the Lord Chancellor *if he were a Bishop*, and in like manner its Paten by the Lord Treasurer *if he were a Bishop*[1]. (*ibid.* ii. 679.) The next rubric provided that if Chancellor or Treasurer were not a Bishop, the King (not the Archbishop) should appoint some Bishop to perform the office in question. (*ibid.*)

In 1236, Ralph de Neville, Bp of Chichester, as Lord Chancellor, carried the *calix lapideus*, at the Coronation of Eleanor, Queen Consort to K. Henry III.; and Hugh de Pateshull, then Canon and Treasurer of St Paul's, but *not as yet called to the office of a Bishop*, carried the paten as Lord High Treasurer. (*Missale Westm.* iii. 1518.) Doubtless a Bishop would have claimed to carry it, if the Coronation had been that of a Sovereign in his own right.

The Stone Chalice and its Paten are not now in existence, having been last used in 1626. The iron-bound treasury chests at the Abbey were broken open by Henry Martin in 1642; and in 1649 the

---

[1] With such authorities only as I have at hand it is impossible to feel quite certain as to the names of those prelates who held the office of Lord Chancellor or that of Lord Treasurer at the moment of a Coronation. So far as I can judge, these at least did so:—

1199. Eustace, Bp of Ely, *Chancellor.*
1377. Adam de Houghton, Bp of St David's, *do.*
1429. John Kempe, Abp of York.
1461. G. Neville, Bp of Exeter.
1483. J. Russell, Bp of Lincoln.
1485. J. Alcock, Bp of Worcester.
1509. W. Warham, Abp of Cant. *do.*
        But he was engaged to anoint and crown the King.
Again:
1308. Walter Reynolds, Bp of Worcester, *Treasurer.*
1327. ?Adam Tarleton, Bp of Hereford, *do.*
1377. H. Wake, Bp of Worcester, *do.*

Regalia at the Tower were "totallie broken and de-faced." The silver-gilt Anointing Spoon, enamelled, and set with four pearls in the shaft, though it is said to be as old as the thirteenth century, was not (we are assured) used as a coronation spoon until 1660[1].

From Lanfranc's time, until 1689, the Archbishop of Canterbury, when unable to anoint the King, deputed the next in dignity, such as the Bishop of London or Winchester, or any other of his choice, to do so[2]. By 1 Will. and Mary, cap. 6, § 2, the Arch-bishop of York may be appointed to administer the oath, or any other Bishop whom the King's Majesty shall appoint. As to sacring, see *Liber Regalis*, where, in the inability of the Abp of Cantèrbury, another prelate "qui inter episcopos tunc presentes dignior re-peritur, aut cui dictus metropolitanus dictum officium velit committere" is named. (*Missale Westm.* ii. 674.) In the case of the vacancy of the see of Canterbury the Chapter of Canterbury claimed the right to select the Prelate to anoint the King. (*ibid.* iii. 1517.)

[The Marshalling of Bishops of the Anglican Communion on the occasion of an assembly at St Paul's Cathedral Church at the conclusion or adjournment of the Lambeth Conference or 'Pan-anglican Synod' of July, 1888, may not improperly

---

[1] L. G. Wickham Legg, *Coronation Records*, 4to. 1901, pp. 191, 388. Cf. *Archæologia*, vol. liii. pp. 118–19; Cyril Davenport, *The English Regalia*, 4to. 1897, p. 30. The Eagle or "Ampull for the Oyle" was ordered in 1660, to replace the Ampulla destroyed. (L. G. W. Legg, u. s. p. 278.)

[2] "*Qui inter episcopos tunc presentes dignior reperitur*," &c. Cf. u. s. p. 82.

find a place here. It will be noticed that the Prelates who hold the dignities in the Provincial Chapter received no special precedence (*as such*) in this general procession "attended by the Members of the Conference, and by the Members of the Lower Houses of Convocation of the Provinces of Canterbury and York, and Members of the House of Laymen of the Province of Canterbury." The Bishops of Durham and Winchester have special precedence, as also the Bishop of London, who on the occasion in question received double honour as being in his own Cathedral Church.]

XXVI. St Paul's Cathedral. *Adjournment of* the Lambeth Conference, July 28, 1888.

ORDER OF PROCESSION.
Virger.
Choristers (two and two).
Gentlemen of the Choir (two and two).
Members of the House of Laymen.
Members of the Lower House of Convocation of the
Northern Province.
Prolocutor of the Convocation of the Northern Province.
Members of the Lower House of Convocation of the
Southern Province.
Prolocutor of the Convocation of the Southern Province.
The Bishops according to the date of their Consecration (Juniors going first).

1. Bishop of Leicester 1888 (July 15).
2. Bishop of Bedford 1888 (July 15).
3. Bishop of Penrith 1888 (May 22).
4. Bishop of Nova Scotia 1888 (Apr. 25).
5. Bishop of Shrewsbury 1888.
6. Bishop of Marlborough 1888.
7. Bishop of Sodor and Man 1887.
8. Bishop of Saskatchewan 1887.

9. Bishop in Jerusalem and the East 1887.
10. Bishop of Edinburgh 1886.
11. Bishop of Clogher 1886.
12. Bishop of Nassau 1886.
13. Bishop in Japan 1886.
14. Bishop of Ely 1886.
15. Bishop of Salisbury 1885.
16. Bishop of Meath 1885.
17. Bishop of Brisbane 1885.
18. Bishop of Niagara 1885.
19. Bishop of Exeter 1885.
20. Bishop of Lincoln 1885.
21. Bishop of Maryland 1885.
22. Bishop of Central Pennsylvania 1884.
23. Bishop of Ripon 1884.
24. Bishop of Qu'Appelle 1884.
25. Bishop of Southwell 1884.
26. Bishop of Chester 1884.
27. Bishop of Kilmore 1884.
28. Bishop of Killaloe 1884.
29. Bishop of North Dakota 1883.
30. Bishop of Huron 1883.
31. Bishop of Central Africa 1883.
32. Bishop of New York 1883.
33. Bishop of Indiana 1883.
34. Bishop of Argyll and the Isles 1883.
35. Bishop of St John's, Kaffraria 1883.
36. Bishop of Aberdeen 1883.
37. Bishop of Truro 1883.
38. Bishop of Llandaff 1883.
39. Bishop of Sierra Leone 1883.
40. Bishop of Mississippi 1883.
41. Bishop of Adelaide 1882.
42. Bishop Coadjutor of Antigua 1882.
43. Bishop of Newcastle 1882.
44. Bishop of Algoma 1882.
45. Bishop of Colchester 1882.
46. Bishop of Barbados 1882.
47. Bishop of Rangoon 1882.
48. Bishop of Pittsburgh 1882.
49. Assistant Bp of Fredericton 1881.
50. Bishop of Singapore 1881.
51. Bishop of Washington 1880.
52. Bishop of Zululand 1880.
53. Bishop of New Mexico 1880.
54. Bishop of North China 1880.
55. Bishop of Jamaica 1880.
56. Bishop of Liverpool 1880.
57. Bishop of Newark 1880.
58. Bishop of New Westminster 1879.
59. Bishop of Michigan 1879.
60. Bishop of Caledonia 1879.
61. Bishop of Travancore and Cochin 1879.
62. Bishop of Wakefield 1879.
63. Bishop of Toronto 1879.
64. Bishop of Ossory 1878.
65. Bishop of North Queensland 1878.
66. Bishop Cramer-Roberts 1878.
67. Bishop of Lichfield 1878.
68. Bishop of Springfield 1878.

69. Bishop of Quincy 1878.

70. Bishop of Newfoundland 1878.

71. Bishop of Pretoria 1878.

72. Bishop of Waiapu 1877.

73. Bishop of Nottingham 1877.

74. Bishop of Rochester 1877.

75. Bishop of Manchester 1876.

76. Bishop of Iowa 1876.

77. Bishop of Bombay 1876.

78. Bishop of Colombo 1875.

79. Bishop of Chicago 1875.

80. Bishop of Cork 1875.

81. Bishop of New Jersey 1875.

82. Bishop of Milwaukee 1874.

83. Bishop of St David's 1874.

84. Bishop of Gibraltar 1874.

85. Bishop of Colorado 1873.

86. Bishop of North Carolina 1874.

87. Bishop of Massachusetts 1873.

88. Bishop Mitchinson 1873.

89. Bishop of South Dakota 1873.

90. Bishop of Moosonee 1872.

91. Bishop of Trinidad 1872.

92. Bishop of Cashel 1872.

93. Bishop of Honolulu 1872.

94. Bishop of Dunedin 1871.

95. Bishop of Grahamstown 1870.

96. Bishop Wilkinson 1870.

97. Bishop of St Asaph 1870.

98. Bishop of Chichester 1870.

99. Bishop of Dover 1870.

100. Bishop of Arkansas 1870.

101. Bishop of Falkland Islands 1869.

102. Bishop of Bath and Wells 1869.

103. Bishop of Carlisle 1869.

104. Bishop of Pennsylvania 1869.

105. Bishop of Auckland 1869.

106. Bishop of Albany 1869.

107. Bishop of Maritzburg 1869.

108. Bishop of Oregon 1868.

109. Bishop of Peterborough 1868.

110. Bishop of Hereford 1868.

111. Bishop of Derry 1867.

112. Bishop of Moray and Ross 1867.

113. Bishop of St Alban's 1867.

114. Bishop of Missouri 1867.

115. Bishop of Maine 1867.

116. Bishop of Nelson 1866.

117. Bishop of Limerick 1860.

118. Bishop of Tennessee 1865.

119. Bishop of Western New York 1865.

120. Bishop Bromby 1864.

121. Bishop of The Niger 1864.

122. Bishop of Quebec 1863.

123. Bishop of Gloucester and Bristol 1863.

124. Bishop of Ontario 1862.
                    [(*Epistoler*).

125. Bishop of Antigua 1860.

126. Bishop of Minnesota 1859.

127. Bishop of Bangor 1859.

128. Bishop Tufnell 1859.

129. Bishop of Columbia 1859.

130. Bishop of Norwich 1857.

131. Bishop Perry 1847.

132. Bishop of Winchester [1864].

133.   Bishop of Durham [1879].

Metropolitans[1].

134. Bishop of Sydney [1884].   135. Bishop of Calcutta [1876].

136. Bishop of Capetown [1874].   137. Bishop of Brechin [1871].

138. Bishop of Rupertsland   139. Bishop of Fredericton [1865].   [1845].

140. Bishop of Guiana [1842].

141. Archbishop of Dublin [1886].

142. Archbishop of Armagh [1886].

Virger.

The Minor Canons of the Cathedral.

Canons' Virger.

The Prebendaries.

Virger.

The Canons Residentiary.

Dean's Virger.

The Dean.

Archbishop's Virger.

Apparitor-General and Secretary and Registrar.

The Archbishop of Canterbury, supported by the Archbishop of York on his right and the Bishop of London on his left.

Their Chaplains.

Bishop of London [1869] (*Gospeller*).   Archbishop of Canterbury [1877].   Archbishop of York [1878].

[1] Only Archbishops and Metropolitans [Nos. 134 and upwards] will have seats in the Sacrarium. Also among them the Bishop of London (Gospeller) has a seat (South), opposite the Primate. And the Bishop of Minnesota [No. 126] as Epistoler, has a seat (South), opposite the Archbishop of York, who sits next to the Primate.

Chaplains of Bishops will in every case follow their Bishops in procession. Seats facing North and South in the Choir Aisles, outside the Sacrarium will be reserved for them. The Chaplains of Archbishops and Metropolitans (to the number of 24) will have seats behind the Bishops within the Sacrarium.

(XXVII.) Conclusion.

We are now in a position to summarise the evidence collected in the foregoing documents.

It appears

(1) That the Prelates sit in Council (as in 1075) in the following order of dignity (nos. ii., iii., xiii.).

		Right	Left		
Other Bishops in Order of Consecration &c. 10, 8, 6	Winton. 4	Ebor. 2	(CANTUAR.) 1	London 3	Other Bishops in Order of Consecration 5, 7, 9, 11, &c.

(2) In case the Archbishop of York is not present :

	Right		Left	
Other Bishops in order of Consecration &c. 10, 8, 6, 4	London 2	(CANTUAR.) 1	Winton. 3	Other Bishops in order of Consecration 5, 7, 9, 11, &c.

(3) In case the Archbishop of Canterbury is absent :

	Right		Left	
Other Bishops in order of Consecration &c. 10, 8, 6, 4	London 2	(EBOR.) 1	Winton. 3	Other Bishops in order of Consecration 5, 7, 9, 11 &c.

(4) In 1075 the order appears to have been :

Heref.	Sarum.	Winton.	Ebor.	CANTUAR.	Lond.	[Coutances]	Worc.
8	6	4	2	1	3	5	7
10. Lincoln		(or		(or		9. Wells	
12. Chichester		Lond.)*		Worc.)*		11. Norwich	
14. Chester		2		3		13. Exon.	

*according to MS.
Canterb. Ff. i . 25 ? de-
rived from Worcester document.

N.B. In 1075, *Durham* was absent,

Rochester see, vacant.

(5)   In consequence of this precedence in Council (as Bp E. H. Browne of Winton suggested (no. i.) in 1886) *London* and *Winton* received respectively the offices of *Dean* and *Subdean* in the Provincial Chapter. But (as he observes) the other capitular prelates (Lincoln, Salisbury, Worcester and Rochester) gained no fresh *precedence*, but ranked according to the date of their consecrations, like the remaining Bishops.

(6)   Salisbury's claim to perform a Royal Marriage at Windsor (in case of the Primate's disability) was *disallowed* in 1121, and Winchester was commissioned to perform the ceremony.   (no. iv.)

[iv.**]   DISCLAIMER BY ROCHESTER OF ANY INVASION OF THE RIGHTS OF SALISBURY.   A.D. 1221.

[BENEDICT DE SANSETUN, Bishop of Rochester, having consecrated Eustachius de Fauconberg for the see of London in 1221, in the vacancy of London and the absence of Sir Pierre des Roches (P. de Rupibus), Bishop of Winchester, writes to disclaim any invasion of the rights of the see of Salisbury, Richard Poore, Bishop of Sarum, having asserted his claim to act as Precentor of the province in a case where the Dean and Subdean of England were unable to act.

This document is entered in three Salisbury collections : *Registrum Rubrum*, fo. 34^b, n. 121, *Liber Evidentiarum*, B. f. xlii, and *Liber Evidentiarum*, C., f. 133 (the best text). It has been edited by Macray in *Sarum Charters*, Rolls' Series, p. 109. In the *Registrum Rubrum* there is (as Mr A. R. Malden informs me) a marginal note in a 15th century hand, not mentioned by Canon Jones and Dr Macray.

On the 25th of April, 1221, Eustace Fauconberg was consecrated Bishop of London (on the vacancy which had occurred through the resignation of William of St Mary church, 25th Jan. 1221) in St Katharine's chapel, Westminster, by

> Benedict de Sansetun, Bp of Rochester (consecrated 20 Feb. 1215),
>
> Jocelin de Wells, Bp of Bath (cons. 1206),
>
> Richard Poore, Bp of Salisbury (cons. 25 Jan., 1215; transl.), in the presence likewise of
>
> William de Cornhull, Bp of Lichfield (cons. 25 Jan., 1215),
>
> Ralph de Wareham, Bp of Chichester (cons. 1218), and
>
> John de Fontibus, Bp of Ely (cons. 1220)[1].

The Bishop of Rochester, who was neither senior by consecration, nor first in episcopal dignity, among those present (but who had been head justice of the four home counties in 1212), performed the part of principal consecrator on this occasion. It may be noted that Hugh de Wells, who had been consecrated to the see of Lincoln in 1209, was not, apparently, named in the commission, although bishops of Lincoln rank as deputies for absent bishops of Winchester; nor was he present on this occasion at Westminster.

The Bishop of Salisbury obtained the following declaration and disclaimer (which I ought to have printed in its chronological position, at p. 14, above).]

---

[1] W. Stubbs, *Registrum Sacrum Anglicanum* (1896), p. 56.

(IV.*) Carta Protestacionis [Benedicti] episcopi
Rofensis *de dignitatibus* Sarr' ecclesie *que
consistunt in consecrandis episcopis, ut preiudicium Ecclesie Sarum non generetur pro aliquo
quod fecit episcopus Rofensis*[1]. (A.D. 1221.)

Omnibvs sancte matris ecclesie filijs presens
scriptum visuris,

B[enedictus], diuina miseracione Rofoñ† ecclesie
minister humilis, salutem in domino.

Cum consecracio venerabilis fratris Eustachii
Londoñ electi J[ocelino] Batoniensi et R[icardo]
Sarr' et ²michi³ B[enedicto] Rofoñ† episcopis,
auctoritate venerabilis patris Pand[ulfi], Dei gracia
Norwyc' electi, domini pape camerarij, tunc apostolice
sedis legati ²in Anglia³ fuisset delegata,

protestante pubplice† R[icardo] Sarr' episcopo
pro ecclesia sua, quod per vacacionem ecclesie
Londoñ, et absenciam venerabilis⁴ P[etri] Wintoñ
episcopi peregre tunc profecti, ad ipsum illa vice
deuoluta fuerit potestas dictum electum consecrandi,
racione cuiusdam antique et diu (ut dicebat) optente⁵
consuetudinis inter episcopos prouincie Cantuariensis,
secundum quam

Londoniensis episcopus decanus
Wintoniensis vero subdecanus
Sarr' autem inter ipsos precentor

perhibetur ;

---

[1] The title printed by Jones and Macray (probably from another
MS.) is :— '*Protestatio Benedicti episcopi Roffensis, se nil in præjudicium
episcopi Sarum fecisse in consecratione Eustachii in ecclesiam Londin-
ensem.*' Sarum Charters, Rolls Series, p. 109.

† *Sic.* ²⁻³ *omitt.* Jones and Macray, *Sarum Charters*, p. 110.
⁴ 'patris' *J. and M.* ⁵ 'obtentæ' *J. and M.*

tandem ex delegacione dicti legati, cum consensu predictorum dominorum episcoporum, illa vice dicto electo munus impendi consecracionis, saluis in omnibus iure et dignitate ecclesie Sarr' in aliorum episcoporum consecracionibus, cum similis[1] casus acciderit.

Et ut ex hac mea consecracione Sarr' ecclesie nullum inposterum generari possit preiudicium, nec[2] ecclesie Rofeñ accrescere, vel Sarr' ecclesie deperire, ego hoc ipsum viua voce sum protestatus, et nichilo-

Reg. *Rub. Sar.* lf. 35.

minus hanc meam protestacionem *ad maiorem securitatem in posterum scripto feci commendari, et sigillo meo communiri.   Testibus

    Johanne [de Fontibus] Helyensi,
    Willelmo [de Cornhulle] Couentrensi,
    Radulfo [de Warham] Cycestrensi, episcopis
    Magistro [Radulfo] archidiacono Cestrensi, et
      Henrico, archidiacono Cant.[3]
    Magistris Thoma de Frakeham[4], et Alexandro,
      tunc officiali domini Cantuari*ensis*, et
    Magistro Luca, canonico Sarr', et multis alijs.
    (Ex *Registro Rubro* Eccl. Sarisburiensis sec.
    xiv. conscripto, f. 34[b]—35, no. 121)[5].

A xvth *century hand has added in the margin:*
  "Nota quod vacante ecclesia London' et absente e[piscopo] Winton', episcopus Sar', vt precentor Anglie, est proximus in dignitate."

---

[1] similiter: *J. and M.*   [2] 'nichil' *Lib. Evid.* C.

[3] Taunton:　*J. and M.* (Henry de Sandford was Archd. of Canterbury, 1202—26, and *Hugh* de Wilton, Archd. of Taunton, about the same date.　For a similar confusion between '*Cant.*' and '*Tant.*' see Hardy, on Le Neve, *Fasti* i. 39 *n.*)　*Lib. Ev.* C. 'Tanton.'

[4] Tramhay: *J. and M.*　('Frakeham,' C. B. *RR.*)

[5] This document appears also in Salisbury *Liber Evidentiarum* B. (*i.e.* the Bishop's copy) n. 121, and *Liber Evidentiarum* C[apituli, cir. A.D. 1300] n. 157.

Also a footnote of like date:

"Episcopus London' est Decanus; Winton, Sub-decanus; et Sar*um*, Precentor."

In the Salisbury Chapter copy of the *Liber Evidentiarum* there is this 15th century marginal note:

"Inter episcopos prouincie Cant[uariensis] episcopus Sar*um* est precentor."

I am not aware whether Hugh de Wells, Bishop of Lincoln, made in 1221 any claim to act, as he might have done, as Vice-chancellor, or substitute for the Bishop of Winchester.

(7) In a vacancy of the see of London (the *Dean*), in ? 1284, or 1303, Winton acts as Subdean, '*tanquam* suffraganeorum Subdecanus.' (no. v.). And in vacancy of Canterbury and London, 'tanquam* Decanus.' (no. ix. § 8, pp. 30, 31.)

* Lyndwood's gloss on '*tanquam*' (p. 21, *supra*) hardly applies here.

(8) In a vacancy of the two sees of London (Dean), and Winton (Subdean), in 1404, *Lincoln* [usually Vice-Chancellor] acts "*tanquam* SS. Cantuariensis Ecclesiæ Cancellarius." (no. vi. pp. 17, 18.)

(9) London is Dean, and acts '*tanquam* Episcoporum Decanus.' It is accordingly his duty to uphold the rights of his Order, when the Primate is absent, according to the Constitution of 1261, as glossed by the canonist Lyndwood in 1433, and to remonstrate, if necessary, with the King himself. (no. viii. p. 21.)

The gloss adds that the Primate has, in his College of Bishops,—

London	for	Dean.
Winchester	„	Chancellor.
Lincoln	„	Vicechancellor.
Salisbury	„	Precentor.
Worcester	„	Chaplain, and
Rochester	„	Cross-bearer. (Nos. vii., viii.)

(10)　Hence I should infer that the Order of Proceeding to the Provincial Chapter would be as follows :

Cross-bearer
(*Rochester*)[1]

Bishops (Junior by consecration, leading)		Bishops (2nd junior by consecration, leading)
Precentor (*Salisbury*)		Vice-chancellor (*Lincoln*)
Chancellor (*Winchester*)	PRIMATE	Dean (*London*)
	Chaplain (*Worcester*).	

(11)　Salisbury is Precentor, and ruler of the choir on solemn occasions, when the Primate celebrates by ancient custom. (nos. vii., xxi.)

(12)　At Enthronization of an Archbishop (as in 1487) Ely (Bp J. Alcock) as Deacon was Gospeller; Rochester, the Crossbearer, Epistoler; Salisbury, the Chanter or Precentor, began the Introit. (no. xi.)

---

[1] N.B.　My authority for placing the *Cruciferarius* (Rochester) at the head of the procession of the Chapter of Bishops, and not immediately before the Primate, is the *special* direction, that Canons walk between the Archbishop and his Cross-bearer, as laid down in *Pontificale Romanum* a Benedicto XIV. recognitum et castigatum, sub auspiciis Pii VII., the *Ordo Recipiendi Processionaliter Prælatum vel Legatum* (long rubric); and *Cæremoniale Episcoporum* Benedicti XIV. lib. II. cap. viii. § 27.　Chr. Marcellus in *Sacræ Ceremoniæ*, Venet. 4°, 1582, lf. 83, 83ᵇ, says that in the time of Sixtus IV. Cardinals went between the Cross and the Pope, but he believed that in earlier times the Pope rode next the Cross.

　　The Reverend E. S. Dewick informs me that the passage in an "*Ordo ad recipiendum processionaliter prælatum vel legatum*"—'Si vero processioni intersint canonici ecclesie cathedralis: illi soli possunt ire post crucem, legati immediate ante eum'—duly appears in the folio Roman Pontifical, Venice, 1520, but that it does not occur in the same *Ordo* of his 14th century manuscript of the Roman Pontifical as arranged by Durandus.　In earlier times (1135) when Rochester was sole chaplain, and not cross-bearer, he followed the Primate. (Gervase, in *X. Scriptt.* i. p. 1587.)

N.B. The then Bp of Ely was Master of the Rolls and Lord Chancellor of England.

(13) At Prince Arthur's funeral (in 1502) Salisbury, with choirmen, sings Mass of the Holy Trinity. (no. xii.)

(14) London ranks next the Archbishop, and is called Dean in the Synod of the Provincial College ; Winton next, carries the pax to the Archbishop, when London celebrates Mass in Synod.

(Similarly when London is absent.   No. ix. § 7, p. 30.)

(15) But when the see of London is vacant, or when the Bp of London is engaged at a distance, Winton acts in his place, and is styled "Subdean." (no. ix. § 7 ; no. xii.) Winton does not, however, act as regards mandates, if London is merely absent, but his see not actually vacant. (no. ix. § 7.)

In 1303, when Canterbury was suspended, and the see of London vacant, Winton consecrated a new bishop for London at Canterbury. (no. ix. § 8, pp. 30, 31.)

In 1308 H. Woodlock (*alias* Segrave), Bp of Winton, crowned K. Edward II. (no. ix. § 9, p. 31). At that date Rob. Winchelsey, the Abp of Canterbury, was suspended, and the see of London was also kept vacant (by appeals to Rome, &c., from 1306 to 1313).

(16) In summoning Convocation, London acts directly (as Dean) under the Archbishop. (nos. xvii., xviii., cf. xvi.)[1]

---

[1] It may be noticed that in the time of Abp Tenison, Dr H. Compton, Bp of London, added his *Recommendation* of the *New Version* of the 'Singing Psalms' by Tate and Brady, 23 May, 1698, to the *Authorization* by William III. in Council, 3 Dec. 1696.

(17)   It is perhaps an open question whether in the case of the mere *absence* of London, Winchester would act in forwarding the mandate concerning Convocation.   It is denied in no. ix. § 7 by Abp Parker (p. 30, *supra*).

(18)   The title of the Bishop of Lincoln in the Provincial College is perhaps the most obscure.   In nos. (xx.) xxi. he is called " Vice-chancellor "; but in nos. xx., xxiii. "Chancellor," and so in modern kalendars and directories, though with some reservation.

The explanation seems to be, that Lincoln stood next in dignity to London and Winchester in the College (though not in the Council), and bore the title ordinarily of Vice-chancellor.   But in the absence of London (the Dean), Winchester (who is Chancellor ordinarily) acted as Vice-Dean, while in his place Lincoln acted as Chancellor *pro tempore*.   Or again when the see of Winchester was vacant, Lincoln was styled Chancellor for the time, and acted *tanquam Cancellarius*.   But Lincoln ought, I think, to be styled merely Vice-chancellor in the directories and kalendars.

(19)   Though in English *Cathedral* Chapters of the Old Foundation (as at Bayeux) the Precentor ranks next the Dean and above both Chancellor and Vice-chancellor ; yet in the *Provincial* Chapter of Bishops he takes only the fourth place, below the Vice-chancellor.

We may infer that, whenever the Chapter of Bishops was fully established, Lincoln was placed above Salisbury, but that Salisbury received the office of Precentor because he chanced to be personally well qualified to rule the choir.   Was the Bishop of that date Richard Poore, or even St Osmund himself? Bishops of Salisbury—we are told by a papist in 1608 (no xiv.)—were recognised in former days as Masters of Ceremonies in the Pope's chapel at Rome, when they chanced to be in that city, and the official *cæremoniarius* made way for them to conduct the musical part of the service. There is no evidence, so far as we are aware, that the Bishop of Salisbury ever shifted from this office in the Episcopal Chapter in the absence of any of his comprovincials. But see his claim to precedence, p. 63. Winton had first been Precentor, p. 81.

(20) Worcester, as Chaplain, ranks next to Salisbury (viii.). A statement to the effect that the arms of the see of Worcester ·bear reference to the Bishop's office in the Provincial Chapter seems untenable. (no. xix.)[1]

(21) Rochester has ranked as a Chaplain among the Suffragans of Canterbury from still earlier days, having latterly the special duty of bearing the Archbishop's Cross in the Episcopal Chapter. (nos. xi., xiii. p. 36, xxi., xxiii. p. 45, *n.*; *cf.* pp. 81—5.)

(22) In Parliament and on great public occasions, after the Archbishops, priority is reserved only to the Bishops of London, Durham, and Winchester. In times when a Bishop sometimes held the office of Secretary of State, he ranked next after the Bishop of Winchester. (no. ix. § 4, pp. 26—8; no. xiii. p. 36; no. xxvi. pp. 60, 61.)[2]

(23) At Coronations the Bishops of Durham and of Bath and Wells have a joint claim to be

---

[1] See Additional Note (F.) p. 82, below.
[2] Privy Councillors (Bps) rank after Durham. *Phillimore*, i. 33.

the supporters of His Majesty (no. xxv. p. 51). Bath and Wells has no special precedence on other occasions.

(24) That the Bishop of London *ex officio* is Preacher at the Coronation is an opinion based by Dean Stanley on insufficient premises, and subsequently abandoned by him, pp. 52, 53 *n.*

(25) Since 1836 the Bp of Oxford has been Chancellor of the Order of the Garter (an office held at earlier periods by Bishops of Salisbury). But he gains no fresh precedence thereby among his brethren.

(26) The late Dr E. Harold Browne, then Bishop of Winchester (in 1886), concluded that at one time his predecessors in that see, being (as now, and since about 1347) Prelates of the Garter, took precedence of all bishops [suffragans of Canterbury and York], and thus became Deans of the Chapel Royal; but that this precedence was lost by statute, 31 Hen. VIII. cap. 10, § 3, which fixed the precedence in Council as stated in § (22), p. 71. Bp Harold Browne, in a letter to Abp Benson, dated Farnham Castle, Surrey, Nov. 16, 1886, maintained that this Statute, though of general application otherwise, did not in the special case of seats in *Synod* overrule the Canonical order stated in nos. (1)—(4), p. 62, above. (It is noticeable that in 1075 the Bp of Durham was not present to maintain the dignity and claims of his see[1].)

---

[1] Ethelwin, the deprived Bp of Durham, died in 1071. The see having been vacant for a year, Walcher his successor was consecrated in March 1071. He was murdered by the mob, 14 May, 1080. He was not present at Lanfranc's councils in 1075; nor in 1072, when Durham was decreed to be subject to York.

Abp Benson was at the time (27 Nov. 1886) inclined to think the Bishop of Winchester's claim substantiated, though he had previously thought otherwise. I have no copy of my reply to him; but it appears from the Order of Proceeding at the time of the great synodical gathering of Anglican Bishops at Lambeth in 1888 (no. xxvi.) that the Bp of Durham was placed after London and before Winchester.

If I may venture to state an opinion, it seems to me that, when an Archbishop or Bishop from another province is introduced among the prelates of Canterbury, then, as York is placed in the honourable position next the Primate of all England, so the Bishop of Durham, who holds a special dignity in the northern province, and who rankèd as a Count Palatine from the days of the Conqueror, should be welcomed to a corresponding place, *i.e.* next to (London) the first in special dignity in the province of Canterbury. In the same way, among Canons in some Cathedral Choirs, Archdeacons have, by long custom (founded originally upon courtesy), had stalls—next to, or among, the *quatuor personae*—assigned to them in consideration of being, what Henry Bradshaw styled them, when within the Cathedral Church, where Archdeacons have no jurisdiction, "the *Bishop's official guests*[1]." So the Bp of Durham is an honoured official guest of the Primate of all England, when he is in the Southern Province.

CHR. W.

---

[1] *Lincoln Black Book*, 8vo. Camb. 1892, p. 107.

SUMMARY OF THE PRECEDING STATEMENTS
AND CLAIMS.

1. CANTUAR.   Prelate in College, and President in Synod.
Crowned the Sovereign, 795, &c., 1087, 1154...
1902 (1100 August, *exiled*), and Queen Consort, Nov. 1100, 1200...1831.

2. LOND.   Dean of the Province, 1162[1], 1175, 1191[2], 1197[3],
1221; '*tanquam*[4] Decanus,' 1261; 1404, 1433
(Lyndwood), 1572, 1705, 1730, 1842, 1874—
1906.
Crowned the King, in absence of Canterbury,
p. 36; Aug. 1100, 1572, 1689.

3. WINTON.   Precentor ('*cantor Cantuariensis ecclesie*'). 1162[1].
But not for some years before 1220.
Subdean, 1221, (?1284), 1303, 1404, 1842.
Dean (in absence of London) 1313, '*tanquam*
Decanus*'; 1572, 1853.
Chancellor, 1433 (Lyndw.), 1572, 1874—1906.
He used to bear the pax to the Archbishop when
London said mass, 1572.
Styles himself '*capellanus vester*,' 1303, perhaps
in courtesy (p. 16).
Crowned the King (in absence of Canterbury
and London), 1308, 1553.

LINCOLN.   Chancellor, 1404 '*tanquam* Cancellarius'; (?)1874,
1893—1904.
Vice-Chancellor, 1433 (Lyndw.), 1572, 1884, &c.
Crowned K. Stephen, 1135.

SARUM.   Claimed to celebrate a royal wedding at Windsor,
1121. *Claim disallowed.*
Claimed to consecrate a bishop of London in
priority to Rochester, 1221.

---

[1] See Appendix (B**.), p. 81, below.
[2] See Appendix (B*.), p. 80, below.
[3] App. (D.), p. 86, below.
[4] "*tanquam*" vere ponitur, non similitudinarie. *Lyndwood.* See
p. 21, *supra*. (But cf. p. 67, *margin*.)

(SARUM, *continued*.)	Claim recognised by Rochester. Precentor, or Chanter (*Rector chori*), 1221, 1433 (Lyndw.); sings introit, 1487; begins mass, 1502; still styled Precentor, 1874—1906. Was formerly recognised as Master of the Ceremonies in the Pope's Chapel at Rome (1608).
WIGORN.	Chaplain, 1191, 1433 (Lyndw.), 1890—1906. (*Not* Treasurer or Sacrist, pp. 41—2.)[1]
ROFFEN.	At first, sole Chaplain, following the Abp, 1140. See Appendix (B.), pp. 79, 80, below. Also, Appendix (B**.), p. 81.—Afterwards :— Cross-bearer, 1433 (Lyndw.), 1572. Cross-bearer and Epistoler, 1487. A Chaplain, 1890—1906. Recognises London, Winton and Sarum as taking precedence, as consecrators, 1221.
ELIENS.	Gospeller in 1487. (This single instance, perhaps, hardly constitutes a valid right.)
BATHON.	At Coronation supports the King on his Majesty's left hand, 1189, 1483 (not 1485), 1626, 1685. (Claim disallowed, 1689, as not made in conjunction with Dunelm.) (1727 *vacant*), 1761, (*not* 1821), 1838, 1902.
ASSAVIEN.	At Coronation of George II. supported his Majesty on the left hand (on the vacancy of the see of Bath and Wells), 1727, p. 51. A SUFFRAGAN's rank, after Earls, Viscounts and Barons; before Chief Justices, Mayor of London, Knights, &c., 1440, p. 32 *n.*
(*a*) EBOR.	See pp. 30, 33 *n.*, 35, 36, 48, 53, 57, 61—2.
(*b*) DUNELM.	See pp. 26, 28, 36, 49, 51, 60, 62. At Coronations, supports the King on his Majesty's right hand, 1189, 1483 (*not* 1485), 1626, 1687 (*claim not made*, 1689), 1727, 1761, 1821, 1838, 1902.
CARLIOL.	Crowned Q. Elizabeth, 1559, under peculiar conditions of Church and State.

[1] There is no evidence that the Provincial Chapter possessed any Ornaments, Vestments, or Treasury, as such.

SINCE THE BEGINNING OF THE XIIITH CENTURY THE POSITIONS AND OFFICES of 4 Bishops in the PROVINCIAL CHAPTER, viz. of :—

London, as Dean
Salisbury, Precentor [1]
Worcester, Chaplain
Rochester, Chaplain *ad crucem* } seem to be undisputed.

Winchester, clearly, *acted as Vice-Dean*, in default of London.

Lincoln, as clearly, *acted as Chancellor*, when both Dean and Subdean were away (1404).

Lyndwood (Canon of Lincoln, Bishop and Canonist), I think, implies that Lincoln would have ranked as Vice-Chancellor only, if London and Winton had been present. This would account for his saying that Winchester is usually Chancellor : but *when London is away*, Winton serves as Subdean, and Lincoln (usually Vice-Chancellor) serves as Chancellor *pro hac vice*. This opinion, however, seems open to debate.

---

[1] In the xiith century (before the building of Salisbury Cathedral church) the Bp of Winchester acted as Precentor (*cantor*) of Canterbury, according to the statement of Gervase of Canterbury. See below, p. 81.

(A.) On Subscriptions, attesting Charters.

It would not be safe to lay too much stress upon the order in which Bishops wrote their attesting signatures to documents about 1090—1150. In the first place, the lists come to us in slightly different order (in some cases) in the various copies in which certain of them have come down to us. Secondly, it is, I believe, common experience, that at the close of a meeting few things are more difficult than to induce a body of men to sign their names to a document in precise order of dignity. At the same time, after analysing the signatures to eight or ten early documents relating to Lincoln and Salisbury in various copies I am convinced that there was a general tendency for the prelates to sign them according to precedence: those three who had special dignities, next the Primate; and the others (as a rule) in order of seniority. It could hardly be expected of a man like St Wulfstan of Worcester, in his 80th year, to be forthcoming so soon as his order came to sign. So he signs lower down. Once, when one archbishop accused him of being illiterate, and the other charged him with insubordination, the saint, instead of going at once to make his answer at the Council which was sitting, astonished his attendants by saying, "Come, we haven't sung our nones! Let us go to service." (Malmesb. *Gesta Pontificum*, iv. § 143, p. 284.)

Another signature in an unusual order is that of another saint—Anselm, Abp of Canterbury—where the signatories (circ. 1094–6) are (1) K. William, (2) T. Ebor., (3) Walkelin Winton., (4) W. Dunelm., (5) Anselm *Cantuar.*, (6) Gundulf Roffen. The business in hand concerned York; so, the Abp of the northern province having signed first, Canterbury brings up the rear with his chaplain Rochester.

But the point to which I would draw attention is, that in the instance in question (Dugdale, *Monast.* vi. p. 1271, no. v.) and in all the other cases of early charters signed by these distinguished prelates, the order almost invariably is for some time after the Norman Conquest[1]: (1) Abp (Cant. *or* Ebor.), (2) Winton., (3) London (*or* Durham, whichever happened to be present). So it is in the Confirmation Charter of benefits and liberties of Lincoln Church usually dated 'Sept. 1090,' but which I am convinced should be, 'after Epiphany 1090–91.' So also in St Osmund's Institution of Dignities and Custom of Salisbury in 1091. So it is again in the 'Oschinton' (Lincoln) Charter of 1095 (Dugd. vi. 1271, no. vi.). In fact the one exception to the priority of Winchester, both to London and Durham, in these early charters, is in a late *inspeximus* (8 Hen. VI.) of the earliest Lincoln Charter of 1090–91 already mentioned, or at least in Dugdale's print of it (*Monast.* vi. p. 1271, no. iv.), where Winchester signs 7th, while in an earlier copy of the same document in the *Registrum Antiquissimum*, he comes 3rd, *i.e.* next after the King and Primate.

But an instance of *London* occurring next after York before the Conquest may be seen in the subscriptions in Wilkins, *Concil.* i. 321.

And such a precedent may have given rise to the answer of his suffragans to Lanfranc in 1073–5 (pp. 5, 8, *supra*), after which the place of London above Winchester was definitely established.

---

[1] I refer to signatures about 1090—95.

(B.) ORDER FOR A CEREMONIAL CROWN-WEARING,
circa A.D. 1140.

It was the custom of Norman Kings, after their
solemn sacring and coronation, from time to time to
be crowned again and wear their crowns at certain
cities[1]. Gervase of Canterbury (who flourished
about 1188) in proceeding in his Chronicle to de-
scribe the ceremonial at the second coronation of
K. Richard I. at Winchester, in 1194, after his
return from captivity (without repetition of the
unction), takes occasion for the benefit of his readers
(seeing that such a thing had not been done since
1158) to narrate the order of a similar second
crown-wearing[2], at Canterbury, by K. Stephen and
his consort, after the accession of Theobald, in 1139,
to the primacy. Gervase had become a monk at
Canterbury in 1163, and he obtained special information for his purpose. At this time, we may
infer, the Bp of Rochester alone among the bishops
acted as the archbishop's chaplain (assisted by two
monks). Subsequently, he became cross-bearer;
and the Bp of Worcester followed the Primate as
his attendant chaplain. In describing the Coronation of Richard III. in 1483, Holinshed relates how
there "went...the abbots and bishops, mitred and
in rich copes; and euerie of them carried their
crosiers in their hands. The bishop of Rochester
bare the crosse before the cardinall," Thomas Bour-
chier, Abp of Canterbury. "The cardinall soong
masse," &c. (Holinshed, *Chron.* iii. 733[b], 744.)

[1] W. Stubbs, *Constit. Hist.* i. 504, 517; ii. 31 (ed. 2, 1875).
[2] At his *sacring*, 1135, no abbots and only two bishops besides the
Primate were present. *Hist. Novella* § 461. (*Gesta Regum*, ii. 539.)

Gervase's note for (?) 1139–40 runs as follows :—

INSTANTE hora tertia, et rege [Stephano] cum baronibus suis et comitibus, quibuslibet preciosis tamen induto vestibus, induantur episcopi et conventus albis et cappis ; et sequentes archiepiscopum Cantuariensem usque ad regis cameram, ordines suos teneant episcopi, secundum primogenita consecrationis ; præter

Eboracensem archiepiscopum, si affuerit,
Lundoniensem,
Wintoniensem, et
Roffensem.

Quorum Eboracensis ad dexteram ibit archiepiscopi Cantuariensis,

Lundoniensis ad sinistram,
Si forte defuerit Eboracensis,
Lundoniensis ibit ad dexteram,
Wintoniensis ad sinistram.

Roffensis vero, qui Cantuariensis archiepiscopi capellanus est, prope archiepiscopum subsequetur a tergo, comitantibus eum a dextris et a sinistris duobus monachis capellanis archiepiscopi, ut cum libro paratus sit ad inveniendas congruas orationes.

Gervase of Cant. *Historical Works*, ed. W. Stubbs (Rolls Series) Lond. 1879, i. 524.

(B*.) Under the date (2 Dec.) 1191 Gervase has a very clear account of the position and duties of the Bishop of London :—

VNDE et episcopus Lundoniensis, qui inter episcopos decanatus præminet dignitate, et ad quem specialiter pertinet ad nutum archiepiscopi, vel Cantuariensis ecclesiæ, episcopos convocare, episcopis Angliæ citatorias misit litteras in hunc modum, &c. (Gervase, *ubi supra*, i. 510.)

(B**.) Notes from Gervase of Canterbury
(A.D. 1162—93).

After the election of Thomas Becket to the primacy in 1162 the right to consecrate him as archbishop was claimed by York (whose petition was unanimously rejected), and likewise by a Welsh bishop who was the senior by date of consecration. In the third place :

Episcopus e contra Roffensis suam esse contendit [benedictionem], quia ab antiquo Cantuariensis ecclesiæ proprius erat capellanus :

Fuerant autem quidam qui pro episcopo Wintoniensi, qui Cantuariensi ecclesia cantoris gaudet officio, allegarent.

Cum autem his diebus Londoniensis vacaret ecclesia, mortuo ejusdem ecclesiæ episcopo, qui ab olitanis temporibus in Cantuariensi ecclesia decanatus præminet dignitate, canonici præ-*fatæ Londoniensis ecclesiæ novo scripserunt electo, suppliciter postulantes quatinus episcopo Wintoniensi liceret in consecratione illa Londoniensis episcopi vices agere, sicut hactenus in minoribus fecerat sacramentis[1].

i. p. 171.

Consenserunt itaque vix tandem episcopi, et consecravit eum Henricus Wintoniensis episcopus,

[1] "Londoniæ quippe episcopali sede, ad quam id pertinere dignoscitur, tunc vacante, Wintoniensis, qui absentis aut non superstitis Londoniensis vices in provincia gerit, id ad se omnimodis pertinere asserebat. At e contra Rophensis, eo quod, ab ecclesiæ suæ fundatione et jure, specialis et peculiaris archipræsulis capellanus sit, id suum esse et non alterius contendebat. Tandem vero...de Rophensis consensu...Henrico Wintoniensi episcopo archipræsulis consecratio est delata." *Vita S. Thomæ* auctore Herberto de Boseham iii. 4. 'Materials' Rolls Series iii. 188.

Dominica octavarum Pentecostes, iij^{tio} nonas Junii [A.D. 1162].

> Gervasii, monachi Cantuariensis, *Opera Historica*, i. 170—71.

In 1190, the Bishop of Ely having been made legate, 'Accessit autem ad eum Gilebertus [Glanvill] Roffensis episcopus, dicens, injuriam factam fuisse Cantuariensi ecclesiæ et sibi, eo quod ipso penitus ignorante aliquis in ecclesia Wigorniensi electus est, cum ipse Cantuariensis ecclesiæ proprius esset capellanus, et dominus archiepiscopus peregre profectus vices suas eidem commendasset.' (Gervase, *u.s.* i. 485.)

The legate, having promised to do justice in the matter, called upon him, at the council held at Westminster in October, 1190, to state his case:—

* i. p. 487. *Cui Roffensis ait : "Quæstiones quidem et querelas habemus ad vos....De consecratione autem rogamus vos ne transgrediatur, id est, ne ab alio fiat quam a capellano Cantuariensis ecclesiæ, nec alibi quam in Cantuariensi ecclesia," &c.

The legate replied, "Consecrationem, et sedem [ad dexteram legati] de qua loqueris, dum archiepiscopus præsens non est, Londoniensi de jure decani sibi vendicare contendit. Præcellit enim cæteris episcopis ut Cantuariensis ecclesiæ decanus."

Roffensis ad hæc : "Quis est hic decanatus, vel quod ipsius officium ? Solummodo ut episcopos vice præconis convocet ad concilium. Sed hoc nichil ad me. Ipse enim ad præceptum Cantuariensis ** p. 488.* metropolitani præconis habet officium. *Roffensis vero, quasi intra septa Cantuariensis ecclesiæ, non

præco sed capellanus est, et vacante ecclesia, vel absente metropolitano, ipsius fere in omnibus vices
exequitur. Unde sedem illius ad dexteram vestram
in hoc concilio expeto, et Wigorniensis electi consecrationem."

The legate then offered the seat to the prior
of Canterbury, who declined it, on the ground that
the primacy was not then really vacant. The prior
and the bishop of Rochester thereupon retired.

The consecration was deferred for a month, and
the place assigned was Canterbury.

" Recognitum est ibidem coram legato simul et
episcopis, Roffensem episcopum Cantuariensis ecclesiæ proprium ab antiquo fuisse capellanum, cum-
que vacante Cantuariensi sede ad vocationem conventus debere Cantuariam accedere, crisma conficere,
et cetera sacramentalia ministrare, eumque in ex-
pensis procurare deberet qui archiepiscopatum custo-
diret. Vivente autem archiepiscopo, sed absente,
vel ægrotante, ad vocationem ejusdem simul et pro-
curationem debet accedere.

Hæc michi, qui hæc scribo, insinuavit idem
Gilebertus Roffensis episcopus, huic matriculæ, ut
verbo suo utar, ad preces ipsius inserenda."

Gervase, u.s. i. 491.

On May 4th, 1191, when the bishops met at
Canterbury, the Bp of Rochester repeated his claim,
in the Archbishop's absence abroad,—"quod omnia
sacramentalia, quæ in ecclesia Cantuariensi facienda
sunt, per manus nostras, sicut per proprium ecclesiæ
capellanum, fieri debeant....Allegat Londoniensis
de jure decanatus sui, sed nichil ad nos. Nullam
enim ei subjectionem debeo, in re nulla obedio, nec

alteri, nisi soli domino meo Cantuariensi archiepiscopo."

He agreed to present the Bishop elect of Worcester to the legate as legate, not as Bishop of Ely. (*ibid.* i. 492.)

K. Richard I. determined to take measures for raising his ransom, and to appoint Hubert of Salisbury to the primacy in 1193. (*ibid.* i. 516.) The bishops were assembled in London for the council, in the absence of the Archbishop of Canterbury elect. To their astonishment, "intravit quispiam crucem bajulans, quem archiepiscopus Eboracensis stupentibus cunctis a tergo subsequens præsumptione stolida turbavit universos." Gilbert of Rochester remonstrated on behalf of the absent primate of all England, and repeatedly declared his appeal to the apostolic see against such an usurpation. Gervase, the chronicler, himself delivered the cross to the new Abp of Canterbury at Lewisham, 3 Nov. 1193. Hubert arrived at Canterbury, 7 Nov., to receive the pall, and during the preparations for his enthronization :—

"Facta est...grandis altercatio inter episcopos, Lundoniensem scilicet et Rofensem, quis eorum in hoc opere videretur esse major. Lundoniensis enim dexteram archiepiscopi, totamque intronizandi solennitatem, suam esse dicebat de jure antiquo, quia Lundoniensis episcopus inter episcopos Cantuariensis ecclesiæ decanatus optinet dignitatem.

E contra Rofensis idem sibi usurpabat, quia capellanus erat.

Quidam [autem] dicebant, quod prioris et conventus esset intronizatio, quia eorum esset electio;

alii dicebant, quod eorum esset intronizatio, quorum
esset consecratio, id *est, episcoporum.

i. p. 523.

Ad sedandam igitur tantorum virorum dis-
sensionem, pro bono pacis, ne tanta solennitas
cassaretur, utrimque provisum est, ut, in susceptione
archiepiscopi, Lundoniensis ejus dexteram optineret,
et in susceptione pallii Rofensis, salva utriusque
debita dignitate.   Lundoniensis¹ vero dixit oratio-
nem cum pallium humeris archiepiscopi imponeretur,
et cum in sede patriarchatus locaretur."

Gervase, *Opera Historica*, i. 522—3.

On the Archbishop of York's cross being carried
erect, but not in the province of Canterbury or in
the presence of the Primate of All England, see
Bp W. Stubbs's introduction to the Chronicle of
Roger Hoveden.   (*Collected Introductions*, p. 278.)
J. Johnson, *Canons*, ed. 1851, ii. 259, s. a. 1279.
Spelman, *Concilia*, ii. 107, 109 (A.D. 1175); 220 (A.D.
1237).

In the Episcopal Register of *Roger de Mortival*
(ii. 201, 247ᵇ) at Salisbury are letters of Archbishops
Walter Reynolds (22 Dec., 1326) and Simon Meopham
(13 June, 1329) *ad interdicendum ecclesias per quas*
[W. de Morton] *Archiepiscopus Eboracensis trans-
ivit, crucem suam ante se faciens baiulari.*

On the Rank and Privileges belonging to the
ARCHBISHOP OF YORK, see Phillimore, *Eccl. Law*
(1895) i. 32.   And on the right of a Bishop, being a
PRIVY COUNCILLOR, to rank next after the Bishop of
Durham, *cf. ibid.* i. 33.

¹ Tandem : *MS.* B.

(C.) A Bishop of Winchester's place as a Baron of the Exchequer, about 1175.

In the *Dialogus de Scaccario* of Richard fitz Nigel, Bp of London, and Treasurer of the Exchequer, written about 1177–88, the places of the Barons and Officers of the Exchequer are detailed. The Chancellor of the Exchequer sat on the chief form or bench (*primum sedile*) to the left of the President (who occupied a place of honour in the middle of the Exchequer). To the right of the President sat the then Bishop of Winchester, Richard Toclive of Ilchester (father of Bp Ri. Poore of Salisbury)—'non ex officio quidem, sed ex novella constitucione, ut scilicet proximus sit thesaurario'—the Treasurer of the Exchequer being placed at the head of the form (*sedile, sive scamnum*) which ran at right angles to the chief bench and at the side of the chamber. W. Stubbs, *Select Charters* (ed. 8, 1905), pp. 177—8, 184.

(D.) The Bishop of London as Dean among the Bishops, A.D. 1197.

In the *Magna Vita* of St Hugh of Lincoln, written about 1200—1235 by his chaplain, Adam, abbot of Eynsham, 1213–28, there is a reference to the Bishop of London as 'Dean among the Bishops' in December, 1197.

Requisito super hoc in coetu illo assensu Lincolniensis episcopi, ipse tacitus secum deliberans paulisper, cum prius tam primas Cantuariensis, quam Londiniensis episcopus Ricardus, qui et decanatus privilegio fungebatur inter episcopos, se suos et sua

regiæ per omnia necessitati exposituros pronuntias-
sent, ita citius respondit, *&c.*

> *Magna Vita S. Hugonis,* ed. Ja. F. Dimock
> (1864), p. 249. Cf. Stubbs, *Select Charters,*
> p. 256.

(E.) THE BISHOPS' PLACES in PARLIAMENT, about A.D. 1250.

Of the *Modus Tenendi Parliamentum* Dr W.
Stubbs (late Bp of Oxford) tells us that this treatise
from which we are about to quote, although its claim
to represent the customs of the time of K. William I.
cannot be maintained, is at least as old as the middle
of the fourteenth century.

" Hic discribitur modus quomodo parliamentum
regis Angliæ et Anglicorum suorum tenebatur tempore regis Edwardi filii regis Etheldredi ; qui quidem
modus recitatus fuit per discretiores regni coram
Willelmo duce Normanniæ, *&c....*

(12°) *De gradibus Parium.* Rex est caput,
principium et finis parliamenti...Secundus gradus est
ex archiepiscopis, episcopis, abbatibus, prioribus per
baroniam tenentibus ; Tertius gradus est de procura-
toribus cleri ; Quartus de comitibus, baronibus, et
aliis magnatibus et proceribus, tenentibus ad valen-
tiam comitatus et baroniæ, sicut prædium est in
titulo [2ᵈᵒ] *De laicis* ; Quintus est de militibus comi-
tatuum ; Sextus, de civibus et burgensibus ; et ita est
parliamentum ex sex gradibus, *&c....*

(14°) *De Inchoatione Parliamenti.* Dominus
rex sedebit in medio majoris banci, et tenetur interesse primo, sexto die parliamenti, *&c....*

(19°) *De Loco et Sessionibus in Parliamento.*
Primo, ut prædictum est, rex sedebit in medio loco
majoris banci, et ex parte ejus dextra sedebit archiepiscopus Cantuariensis, et ex parte ejus sinistra
archiepiscopus Eboraci, et post illos statim episcopi,
abbates et priores linealiter, semper tali modo inter
prædictos gradus et eorum loca, quod nullus sedeat
nisi inter suos pares ; et ad hoc tenetur senescallus
Angliæ prospicere, nisi rex alium assignaverit ; ad
pedem regis dextrum sedebunt cancellarius Angliæ
et capitalis justiciarius Angliæ, et socii sui, et eorum
clerici qui sunt in parliamento ; et ad pedem ejus
sinistrum sedebunt thesaurarius, camerarius, et
barones de scaccario, justiciarii de banco, et eorum
clerici qui sunt de parliamento."

W. Stubbs, *Select Charters*, ed. 8, Oxon. 1905,
pp. 502—11 ; from Sir T. Duffus Hardy's text.
Cf. Camb. Univ. Lib. MS. Mm. iii. 29.   There is
a 16th or 17th cent. MS. '*Modus tenendi Parliamentum* (per vetustissimum authorem). Hic scribitur
modus...' at Trin. Coll. Cam. MS. O. 10. 11 (2).
In 1572 John Hooker (*otherwise* Vowell) compiled
*The Order and Usage of Keeping the Parlements
in England*, 4to [? Exeter].   In 1628 T. Walkly
printed *The Order and Manner of the Sitting of the
Lords Spiritual and Temporall*, 4to ; and, in 1639–
40, *Catalogues of the Dukes*, &c.   In 1641 (and again
in 1659 and 1671) W. Hakewill of Lincoln's Inn
edited the *Modus tenendi Parliamentum*.   Sir T.
Smith's [*Authority,*] *Form and Manner of holding
Parliaments* was printed in 1685, 12mo.   (He died
in 1577 ; his *De Republica Anglorum* appeared in
1584, &c., 4to.)

(F.) THE ARMS OF THE SEE OF WORCESTER.
Cf. pp. 41—2, § (20), *supra.*

Through the kindness of Dr T. A. Blyth who
has edited the *Worcester Diocesan Church Calendar*
since 1889, I am enabled to add, that the note about
the Arms of the See of Worcester (which are herald-
ically described as, "Argent ten torteaux in pile")
had not appeared in the earliest issues of this almanac
from 1861 to 1867, beyond a plain and intelligible
statement of their blazon. In 1868 the additional
words (about the Bp of Worcester celebrating before
the College) which I have cited on p. 41 *n.*, above,
were introduced, and were retained in subsequent
years until 1875. But in 1876 the words thus added
were omitted, possibly in deference to Dr Benson's
criticism, which I may have passed on to someone
in authority. In 1899, when a new block to represent the shield was introduced, from a sketch made
by himself, Dr Blyth enlarged the amended (or cur-
tailed) footnote as follows :—

" The Arms of the See of Worcester, like those
of the See of Hereford, were assumed from the
personal Arms of one of its Bishops. The date of
the introduction of these Arms appears to be un-
known, but it is almost certain that they were
derived from the Coat of Arms of Godfrey[1] Giffard,
Bishop of Worcester (1268–1302), cousin of King
Edward I. They were adopted as the Arms of the
See after the Bishop's death. The first known
Episcopal Seal on which these appear as Diocesan
Arms is that of Bishop Thomas Peverell (1407–

---

[1] 'Godfred' :—*Calendars for* 1899—1902.

1419). They are there impaled with his personal coat. The Torteaux (painted in scarlet on the silver shield) have been supposed to represent wafers used at the Holy Eucharist."

Welcoming an expert herald and antiquary in the present Bishop of Worcester (the Right Reverend Huyshe Wolcott Yeatman-Biggs, D.D.), Dr Blyth, while preparing the issue of the Calendar for 1906, obtained from his Lordship, not only the more scientific description of the blazon cited at the beginning of the present note, but an observation to the effect that their supposed reference to Eucharistic wafers "is doubtful, as the wafers are white; moreover, some heralds call the Torteaux 'hurts,' or wounds[1], hence their colour."

It is gratifying to find the opinion of Chancellor (subsequently, Archbishop) Benson thus authoritatively corroborated.

(G.)   Of Bishops Suffragan.

Immediately upon his appointment to the See of Lincoln in 1869, my Father noted in his diary a few designs which he considered to be "*Agenda* σὺν Θεῷ," and which he kept constantly in his prayers. But *sans écrire* came the provision of a Bishop for Nottingham. Already the "Increase of the Episcopate" had been near his heart for many years. The formation of a separate new diocese in the then temper of Parliament and the judgement of advisers of the Crown was not in those days con-

---

[1] *Hurts*, however, are *azure*; and, "by some, supposed to represent the hurtleberry." (*Ogilvie.*) An allusion to Hartlebury Castle seems improbable in early heraldry.

sidered to be as yet within the range of practical policy ; but the Act 26 Hen. VIII. (c. 14)—though disused since the times of Richard Barnes, 1st Suffragan of Nottingham, 1567–70 ; Richard Rogers, Dean of Canterbury, 3rd Suffragan of Dover, 1569–97[1] ; and John Sterne, 2nd Suffragan of Colchester, 1592–1608—was still remaining upon the Statute Book since 1536. The Bishop of Lincoln revived the activity of this long dormant statute by moving for the appointment of a Bishop Suffragan for Nottingham ; and Dr Henry Mackenzie was consecrated in February, 1870, and held the office till his resignation in 1877, dying in the following year. In 1877 Dr Edward Trollope became 3rd Suffragan Bishop of Nottingham (counting the Elizabethan Dr Barnes). By his liberality and his archæological and architectural taste he contributed substantially to the preparation of the collegiate buildings at Southwell to become the cathedral church for the diocese of Notts, and (as appears from Crockford's *Directory*) he retained the title of "Bishop Suffragan of Nottingham" in the early years of Dr King's episcopate (1885, &c.) at Lincoln after my Father's resignation and death, which occurred after Dr Ridding's consecration in 1884 as first Bishop of the Diocese of Southwell, for which in its turn Dr Ridding procured a "Bishop Suffragan of Derby" in 1889.

[1] Dr Rogers was usually styled "My Lord of Dover" in the Chapter Acts, &c. Twenty-six places were named in the Act of 26 Hen. VIII. as "the Sees of Bishops Suffragan." To these the Act 51 & 52 Vict. permit additions to be made under Order in Council, also a change of "See" for a Bishop consecrated under one of the older titles. (*Crockford.*)

On May 22nd, 1874, the Right Honourable R. A. Cross, H.M. Secretary of State, addressed a letter to the Archbishop of Canterbury, stating the opinion of the Law Officers that the proper *signature* for a Suffragan Bishop, consecrated under the Act of 1535, was his Christian name (or one of such names), followed by the name of his see, such as "Ri. Dover." The clerical *status* of such a Bishop was considered to depend upon the fact of his acting or not acting at the time under a commission from a Diocesan Bishop. In the former case, and within the limits of his jurisdiction, "his *status* is probably next to that of the Bishop for whom he is acting. But elsewhere, or when not acting under any commission, he can only rank according to the date of his consecration, with other persons, whether colonial or others, who may have been consecrated to episcopal functions."

The letter here quoted has been printed in Crockford's *Clerical Directory* (*e.g.* for 1890, pp. lxvi, lxvii), with the addition of a statement as to the correct "*style and title*" of Bishops Suffragan.

"There is ample documentary evidence that the predecessors of the present Bishops of Dover and Nottingham were up to the disuse of their office in the reign of James I., every whit (whether by right or courtesy) as much 'Lord Bishops' as the Diocesans, Peers of Parliament, whose labours they shared and lightened."

In 1883, when, through the munificence of the Bishop of Lincoln and others, the prospect of the foundation of a separate see of Southwell (for Nottinghamshire, and Derby) to have a *Diocesan*

Bishop, a *Suffragan of Canterbury*, was approach-
ing realisation, some friends of Dr Trollope (the
" Bishop Suffragan," under Lincoln) presented him
with a beautiful pastoral staff.   The following letter,
doubtless, in part concerns the propriety of its use.

DR E. W. BENSON, ARCHBISHOP OF CANTERBURY,
TO DR CHR. WORDSWORTH, BISHOP OF LINCOLN.

> LAMBETH PALACE, S.E.
> 14 *Ap.*, 1883.

MY DEAREST LORD BROTHER,

I followed your counsel, and took the
legal opinion of the Vicar-General on the qu[estio]n
of suffragan B[isho]ps sitting in the Upper House.

It was exactly what you would yourself have
expected.   But the question was not brought up
to us.

I do not doubt that you are quite right as to the
bearing of crosiers before B[isho]ps suffragan[1].   It

---

[1] According to *Pontificale Romanum* (De Consecratione Electi in
Episcopum) '*consecratus...surgit, et accedens cum mitra*, et baculo
pastorali *ante medium altaris...dicit*, Sit nomen Domini benedictum.'
ed. Rom. 1818, p. 84.   Further, *Ceremoniale Episcoporum*, lib. i.
c. 17 § 5, ' Utitur...Episcopus baculo pastorali in sua tantum Civitate,
vel Diœcesi, et etiam alibi, ex permissione loci Ordinarii, et ubi
consecrationes, aut ordinationes, vel benedictiones personales facere,
ipsi Apostolica auctoritate conceditur.
§ 6.   Utitur autem in omnibus Processionibus, quæ si longioris
viæ fuerint, faciet illum ante se immediate deferri a ministro, qui
de eo servit...Si vero Processionis via fuerit brevis, poterit ipsemet
Episcopus sinistra manu illum deferre.' ed. Venet. 1837, pp. 61—2.
The question, whether a 'Suffragan' Bishop (i.e. a Diocesan
Bishop) should use his staff in presence of his Archbishop Metropolitan,

surely could not be his *own* staff, but must be his principal's staff, if instance of its use occur.

I suppose a suffragan could "celebrate pontifically." If so, does he bear a crosier for the benediction? If so, *why*?

We congratulate you most lovingly on Mrs Wordsworth's birthday—and we wish you both many a happy return of it—free from anxiety and suffering.

We understood—but we greatly deplored your absence from Convocation.

How is a boy archbishop to escape doing and

was treated by Paris de Grassis as one long before under discussion. *De Cæremoniis Cardinalium* i. 8, fo. 6ᵇ. ed. Venet. 1582.

The Pope of Rome 'ne porte point de crosse; mais il prend, en certaines occasions, la grande croix [qui ne porte point la figure du Sauveur] différente de la croix papale [qui n'a point deux traverses comme celle des Patriarches]...La crosse, recourbée dans sa partie supérieure, est l'emblème d'une jurisdiction bornée, dit Innocent III.; la jurisdiction du Pape n'a pas de limites.' *Election et Couronnement du Souverain-Pontife*, Paris, 1846, pp. 128—9. In illustrations to Marcellus *De Cæremoniis S. Rom. Eccl.* Junta, 1582, only on fo. 20 is there any representation of a curved pastoral staff, where the prelate consecrating the newly elected pope to the episcopate kneels and holds it ('*crucem*,' the text says) when his Holiness is blessing the people. According to Innocent III. St Peter handed his staff to Eucharius of Trêves; so his successors do not receive one at enthronement. J. B. E. Pascal, *Rational Liturgique* (Migne, 1844), p. 145.

In the Register of Roger de Mortival at Salisbury (ff. 201, 247ᵇ) are entered monitions from Walter Reynolds (22 Dec. 1326) and Simon Meopham (13 June, 1329) Abps of Canterbury, interdicting churches where W. de Melton, Abp of York, had his cross borne before him in the Southern province. See above, p. 85.

I have ascertained that in fact Dr E. Trollope, while Bishop Suffragan of Nottingham, caused his pastoral staff to be borne before him by a chaplain in Southwell Minster. But this, I suppose, was not in the presence of a superior. He wore his episcopal ring, and presented his hand to be kissed by those whom he admitted to holy orders.

suffering mischiefs unless his fathers will come and counsel him ?   It cannot be.

Your most loving

and observant orator[1],

ED. C.

[1] *Orator* :—This, no doubt, was mutual.

My Father had, hanging up at Riseholme, a framed lithograph, representing the south east view of St Mary's Church, Truro, as it then stood, before the Cathedral Church was built on to the sixteenth-century south aisle—the most interesting feature preserved from the old parish church.   This picture had been given him by Dr Benson, who was then leaving the Chancery at Lincoln for Lis Escop in Cornwall, and the newly founded diocese of Truro, and who had written the date, and a text from Canticles viii, beneath the sketch— " M DCCC LXXVII : *Orate Vos pro Sorore Parvula.*"

O ἡγούμενος
ὡς ὁ διακονῶν.

Sec. Luc. xxii. 26–7.

Printed in the United States
By Bookmasters